Activity-Centered Design

Acting with Technology
Bonnie Nardi, Victor Kaptelinin, and Kirsten Foot, editors

Activity-Centered Design

An Ecological Approach to Designing Smart Tools and Usable Systems

Geri Gay and Helene Hembrooke

The MIT Press
Cambridge, Massachusetts
London, England

© 2004 Massachusetts Institute of Technology

All rights reserved. No part of this book may be reproduced in any form by any electronic or mechanical means (including photocopying, recording, or information storage and retrieval) without permission in writing from the publisher.

This book was set in Sabon by Graphic Composition, Inc., Athens, Georgia, and was printed and bound in the United States of America.

Library of Congress Cataloging-in-Publication Data
Gay, Geri.
  Activity-centered design : an ecological approach to designing smart tools and usable systems / Geri Gay and Helene Hembrooke.
    p. cm. — (Acting with technology)
  Includes bibliographical references and index.
  ISBN 0-262-07248-3 (hc. : alk. paper)
  1. Human-computer interaction. 2. System design. 3. Human-machine systems—Design. I. Hembrooke, Helene. II. Title. III. Series

QA76.9.H85G39   2004
                                                                              2003059287

10 9 8 7 6 5 4 3 2 1

This book is dedicated to R. V. T., whose visionary thinking, generosity of support and encouragement, and youthful curiosity have enabled us to think big, take chances, and continue to do what we do best.

Contents

Series Foreword

The MIT Press Acting with Technology series is concerned with the study of meaningful human activity as it is mediated by tools and technologies. The goal of the series is to publish the best new books—both research monographs and textbooks—that contribute to an understanding of technology as a crucial facet of human activity enacted in rich social and physical contexts.

The focus of the series is on tool-mediated processes of working, playing, and learning in and across a wide variety of social settings. The series explores developments in postcognitivist theory and practice from the fields of sociology, communication, education, and organizational studies, as well as from science and technology studies, human-computer interaction and computer-supported collaborative work. It aims to encompass theoretical frameworks including cultural-historical activity theory, actor network theory, distributed cognition, and those developed through ethnomethodological and grounded theory approaches.

This book makes the case for activity-centered design, employing activity theory as a base but also venturing into theoretical traditions such as configural analysis to localize the critique and design of particular technologies. The analyses of technologies such as wireless devices and software for museum and campus tours are rooted in activity theory, but each extends beyond the broad framework of activity theory to specialized theories dealing with, for example, educational practice or the use of physical space—exactly the way activity theory must be used in practice. Activity-centered design is an exemplary application of activity theory, showing its use across a broad range of technologies the authors analyze and design.

The authors are specialists in computer-mediated communication, and they apply this lens expertly to their analyses. They provide a cogent critique of wireless technology in the classroom, based on detailed empirical findings. Through careful analysis of logs and interviews, the authors discovered serious problems of fragmented attention and the dissolution purposes of the technology. The authors draw together the threads of computer-mediated communication (CMC) analysis with activity theory in this analysis, observing that there is a "need for researchers to look at tools in relation to one another—that is, to the relationship between face-to-face communication and mediated communication spaces and to the relationship among the different applications that are available through wireless communication tools."

The authors expand notions of evaluation, observing that "evaluation activities are embedded in complex technosystems and cannot be isolated from the system under study." They note that simple metrics, such as the number of hits on a Web site, may reveal little and that activity-centered analysis is necessary to achieve deeper understanding. The authors critique standard notions of user-centered design, urging us to adopt a framework in which we consider the multiplicity of groups and individuals engaged in the use of technology. Most important, the authors provide candid critiques of their own technological designs, following their users in detail over time and getting to the bottom of their user experiences. This is something we can all learn from the HCI and CSCW communities.

This book returns many gifts to the reader. It shows how to apply activity theory fruitfully, offers new tools and perspectives for evaluation, and sets a standard for frank assessment of the tools that we design as they are used in everyday activity. The editors warmly recommend this book to you and welcome it to the Acting with Technology series.

Preface: Mediating Interactions

My first experience with using technology as a mediation tool occurred in 1980. I was working on my master's degree at the time and had decided to use the new technology of portable video as an intervention tool to help resolve a community conflict in eastern Maine. I had grown up in this coastal region, so I knew it well.

Beginning in 1979, a number of Maine citizens had begun protesting the spraying of blueberry barrens by blueberry growers and the spraying of hardwood trees by pulp and paper companies. By the summer of 1980, the positions held by the protesters and the businesspeople (blueberry growers, processing factories, and pulp and paper industry) were polarized. The protesters felt that business interests controlled the major media outlets, which therefore did not publicize any positions that were against spraying, and also that state officials and regulatory agencies were not addressing their concerns about the dangers of pesticides. The long dispute had escalated to the point where the protesters were threatening to shoot down spray planes and helicopters and to use other means to stop chemicals from coming into the region. These threats led the two sides to a court battle in the summer of 1980.

Protesters were especially upset about a crop duster that had flown on a windy morning and sprayed 245T (a component of Agent Orange), which drifted onto gardens, onto trees, and into a river where 20 percent of Atlantic salmon spawned. In July, state officials flew to this community to reassure residents that the spray would not harm them, their food, or their water supply, but these reassurances proved to be less than persuasive when an elderly woman offered the state officials a tomato from her garden, and no one would eat it.

As an earnest graduate student who was exploring the effects of using video as a mediation tool in this community conflict, I met separately with state officials, some of the leaders of the protest groups, and representatives of the businesses and explained the proposed plan. I would teach the protesters and businesspeople to videotape messages that I would then show to the other participants. I assured protesters, factory owners, and growers that they would control the messages and that nothing would be shown without their permission. Finally, I told them that I was attempting to remain neutral because I needed to gain the trust and participation of both sides to encourage communication and dialogue.

Looking back on this experience, I am amazed that two such polarized groups agreed to participate in the video mediation process. The portability of the video tool meant that I was able to talk with people in their own familiar environments, and the medium allowed them to control the messages. On some level, both parties felt that they had control of the process.

After the first few rounds of making and viewing tapes with these groups, I wondered whether the process was actually making the situation worse. Each side seemed to want only to express and reinforce its own point of view. The growers and owners did not want to change their practices, which continued to frustrate the protesters.

After six weeks, I realized that I was becoming an unofficial expert on the controversy. People on both sides starting asking me for information that I had gathered from the articles, papers, and other documents that I was collecting for my research. I was the only source for various government and unofficial publications about the relevant herbicides and pesticides and the standard regulations for their use. Although I struggled to remain neutral about the situation, my research indicated that some of the practices that I observed were questionable. One morning, for example, I saw a plane empty unused chemicals onto the edge of the airstrip that bordered a river, thus potentially polluting the river and the ecosystem that it supported.

A major turning point in the controversy occurred when after one court session, the wife of a major blueberry grower asked whether the growers' wives could join their husbands at the next viewing of the protesters' tapes. At that viewing session, the wives asked their husbands whether any of the protesters' concerns were valid: Did the husbands not care about the health of their children and grandchildren? Were any of the organic methods for controlling weeds and pests viable? Shouldn't they look into it? The permanency of the video recordings allowed new audiences to bring new or fresh perspectives to the same dialogue.

Through the easily used and accessible technology of the video mediation process, each side on the pesticide controversy could present its position fully, develop multilevel understandings of the other side's concerns, and come up with constructive solutions. Eventually, representatives from both sides of this highly charged issue were able to meet face to face.

Using technology tools to enhance communication and to develop shared understandings has been a sustained interest of mine for over twenty years. Even as media technologies have changed greatly, the underlying issues of access, participation, creativity, and control regarding communication technologies have remained remarkably the same. And as my colleagues, my graduate students, and I research the uses and designs of technologies, we continue to be intrigued by the fundamental challenges and possibilities of context-based design of mediated environments.

Geri Gay
Ithaca, New York

Acknowledgments

This book represents the combined efforts of many researchers and designers who have worked in the Human-Computer Interaction Group at Cornell University from 1990 to the present. In addition, a number of agencies, foundations, and individuals funded the interdisciplinary research, evaluation, and design studies described in this volume, including IBM, IBM-Japan, Intel, the National Science Foundation, the AT&T Foundation, and the Mellon Foundation. In particular, we would like to acknowledge the following individuals for their contributions: Tammy Bennington, Kirsten Boehner, Jenna Burrell, Hichang Cho, Nicholas Farina, Laura Granka, Michael Grace-Martin, Julian Kilker, Kiyo Kubo, Jae-shin Lee, Tara Panella, Wendy Martin, Joan Mazur, Robert Rieger, Amanda Sturgill, David Sturgill, Michael Stefanone, and Jeff Yuen.

We also thank Kirsten Boehner, Jeffrey Hancock, Deborah Trumbull, and Joseph Walther for reviewing the manuscript and making many helpful suggestions for its improvement. A special thank-you goes to Nathaniel Stern for creating the "wire guys" that appear on the cover.

Introduction: Making the Case for Context-Based Design

This book documents our efforts toward articulating what we consider to be a significant shift in human-computer interaction (HCI) design. We are convinced that the shift from user-centered design to context-based design corresponds with recent developments in pervasive, ubiquitous computing networks and in the appliances that connect with them, which are radically changing our relationships with personal computing devices. Additionally, this shift signals a "coming of age" of theoretical frameworks such as activity theory (Kapetelinin, 1996; Leont'ev, 1978; Nardi, 1996a, 1996b; Vygotsky, 1962; Wertsch, 1991) and social construction of technology theory (Pinch & Bijker, 1987), which attend to the sociohistorical contexts of technology use and human activity.

One shift that we have observed is from a focus on human-computer interaction to a focus on human interaction that is mediated by technology in context (Nardi, 1996a, 1996b). We use the concepts of activity theory and related theories and methods to help ground and illuminate ongoing interactions among the uses of computer systems, the practice of design, and the evaluation of designs. With this coming of age, we believe that it may be time to develop models that specifically support both research and development and to support empirical, contextual investigations of human-computer interactions in the ubiquitous computing environments enabled by these networks.

In this volume, we report on the research that we have completed on the use of technologies in everyday contexts and over time. We implement new methods for understanding users' behaviors and motivations as they interact with technology in context, and we then apply these findings to the design of new technologies. We develop the following main points in this book:

• *User centered to user involved*   Where once we focused on what we thought users should do, we now begin the design process with an understanding of what people already do. Users need to be involved at the grassroot level of the design process, and designers and researchers need to attend to the situations in which tools will be used.

• *Laboratory to context*   Within this particular theoretical ecology, the emphasis on understanding specific needs and behaviors of individuals has evolved to an emphasis on understanding the activities and the meaning of those activities in social and networked contexts. Technology that is introduced into an organization or environment changes that situation. Likewise, technologies and organizations are in the process of ongoing change. Designers need to understand these dynamic processes within their particular environment or context.

• *Rigid to emergent design practices*   Step-by-step design procedures usually do not work in complex, messy situations of use. To design robust, suitable, and workable systems, the design process needs to be flexible, adaptive, and rooted in real experience.

• *Individual to groups*   Performing virtually any task in a work environment is fundamentally social and involves cooperation and communication with others.

• *Bounded activities to cross-boundary tasks*   Many tasks that use computers cut across time and space dimensions. Students who use computers in classrooms can also communicate with friends, trade stocks, and shop online. More people are working at home and managing personal affairs at work. The portability of wireless computers and other digital devices also allows for flexibility and accessibility across temporal and spatial boundaries.

As we articulate various aspects of context-based design, we discuss how various projects, research studies, and design challenges were parts of an evolving system of ideas about users, designers, design tasks, and user tools. Some of our discussion of context-based design is historical, but the key objective here is to provide contemporary insights into the vitality of our design approach and research studies. In essence, we have been socially constructing, annotating, and reflecting on our own practice in an iterative, "technologically textured" (Ihde, 1991, p. 1) way.

In chapter 1, Activity Theory and Context-Based Design, we examine specific ways that the activity-theory framework can inform the design and use of technology. The core ideas of activity theory have been described in many other places (Engeström, Miettinen, & Punamäki, 1999; Kuutti, 1996; Leont'ev, 1978; Nardi, 1996a, 1996b; Werstsch, 1991). In our work on human-computer interaction, we attempt to explicate the workings of communicative tools, spaces, and practices and thereby raise numerous questions regarding the activity of design. How do tools mediate activities? Do different kinds of tools mediate differently? How do we make visible and represent multiple, simultaneously occurring processes? As in any mediated sociocultural context, the relationship between the activity and the tool is a reciprocal one. In chapter 1, we begin to explore how activities shape the requirements of particular tools and how the application of the tool begins to reshape dimensions of activity throughout an iterative design process.

In chapter 2, Understanding Perspectives: Social Construction of Technology, we investigate the conceptions, power relationships, motives, goals, and structures within the context of integrating wireless mobile devices into museums. Using a concept-mapping tool, we found few areas of agreement among various stakeholders regarding the functions that were needed to create, use, and maintain mobile computing technologies in museums. Museum staff, designers, and patrons constructed the idea of using mobile computers in partially overlapping and partially conflicting ways that reflected their different backgrounds. Throughout the needs-assessment and pilot phases, roles were reassigned, rules were changed, and structures were reinterpreted. Finally, using the social construction of technology (SCOT) framework, we found that stakeholders held distinct needs and goals that needed to be acknowledged during the design process so that groups could reach closure or consensus.

Despite the many studies and technological innovations for supporting mediated conversations researchers have a very imperfect understanding of what works and what does not work in online environments. We do know that people have difficulty using virtual reality and other complex systems (Erickson, Halverson, Kellogg, Laff, & Wolf, 2002). The design of collaborative virtual environments (CVEs) is known to affect the ways that we communicate and employ social conventions. The presence of others online, the way that objects are organized, and other design factors afford certain ways of responding to others in virtual spaces. In chapter 3, Creating a Sense of Place: Designing for Online Learning Conversations, we describe ways of incorporating social cues or structures that are useful in supporting learning conversations online.

The two-year study described in chapter 4, Blurring Boundaries: A Study of Ubiquitous Computing, was designed to elicit feedback regarding the usefulness, usability, and desirability of mobile computing devices for students' activities. Mobile computers can potentially transform the activities of learning, researching, and communicating. Understanding computer-mediated activities via an activity-theory approach further requires an understanding of a social-historical context—that is, how activities and mediating devices emerge from particular cultures and practices, from particularities of the situated actions, including peoples' needs and goals, and from the activity itself (Lave & Wenger, 1991; Nardi, 1996a, 1996b; Nardi & O'Day, 1999).

In chapter 5, Designing for Context-Aware Computing, we describe the iterative design of wireless communication networks and context-aware computing systems. Context-aware computing is a field of study that researchers have just begun to explore. Only a few concrete applications have been built and tested. The idea behind context-aware computing is that the users' environment—including where they are, who they are with, and what they are doing—can inform the computing device. This added knowledge changes the interactions between user and device. Because individuals associate places with events and activities, the information and tasks presented to the user can be filtered for their location. Wireless devices help mediate activities and create a system of distributed cognition. Where user-centered design and analysis seem inadequate to understanding the complexities of system use in such new social networked environments, activity theory begins to shed some light.

In the final chapter, Configural Analysis of Spaces and Places, we present our ideas on how computer spaces, real and virtual, might be analyzed to gain fresh new insights into ubiquitous computing behavior. In earlier chapters, we focus on the tools, the activities they invoke, and the context in which these activities take place. In this chapter, the focus instead is on what the actual spatial map or layout of the computing space might look like and how the layout might be analyzed to predict movement, function, and social interactions within that space. We borrow heavily from architecture's configuration theory and its techniques for extracting and visualizing these recurrent patterns based on the relation of spaces within larger spaces. We outline the theory, identify the indices that quantify space, and explore how some of our own datasets might be analyzed using what Bill Hillier (1996) and others refer to as nondiscursive analysis.

Activity-Centered Design

1

Activity Theory and Context-Based Design

Introduction

A significant evolutionary shift has occurred in human-computer interaction (HCI) design. Prior to this shift, computer software designers tended toward a computer-centered design approach that at best assumed and at worst ignored the needs and preferences of end users. This approach prioritized the attributes of the technology itself and often resulted in design solutions that were in search of problems. Its limitations gave rise to a human-centered design in which users articulated their needs and developers observed or listened to users and then addressed various needs in their designs. Unlike the technology push of computer-centered design, human-centered design emphasizes human needs and objectives and the technology that serves these purposes.

Another shift has begun now—to a context-based design where the use, design, and evaluation of technology are socially co-constructed and mediated by human communication and interaction. Context-based design builds on human-centered design by positioning the interactions between users and mediating tools within the motives, community, rules, history, and culture of those users. In addition, context-based design calls for designers and evaluators to reflect on the elements of their own context and on the way that this space interacts with the space of technology use.

This book uses activity theory as an orienting framework for context-based design. In our work on human-computer interaction, we attempt to explicate the workings of communicative tools, spaces, and practices and thereby raise numerous questions regarding the activity of design. How do tools mediate activities? Do different kinds of tools mediate differently?

How do we make visible and represent multiple, simultaneously occurring processes? As in any mediated sociocultural context, the relationship between the activity and the tool is a reciprocal one. Activities shape the requirements of particular tools, and the application of the tool begins to reshape dimensions of activity. We use the concepts of activity theory and related theories to help ground and illuminate this ongoing interaction between the uses of computer systems, the practice of design, and the evaluation of designs produced.

Activity Theory: An Overview

Activity theory draws inspiration from the work of the Russian semiotician and psychologist Lev Semenovich Vygotsky (1962), who argued against artificial separations between mind and behavior and between mind and society. Contrary to the dominant mentalist tradition of his time, Vygotsky posited the unity of perception, speech, and action. In addition, he emphasized the centrality of mediating devices, such as language and other symbols or tools, in the development of mind and thought. The emphasis on meaning through action, the connection between the individual and the social, and the role of mediating tools provide the kernel around which activity theory has developed.

Building on these principles, Alexei N. Leont'ev (1981) created a formal structure for operationalizing the activity system as a complex, multilayered unit of analysis (figure 1.1). His model is less a representation of reality than a heuristic aid for identifying and exploring the multiple contextual factors that shape or mediate any goal-directed, tool-mediated human activity.

As indicated by Engeström's (1999a) model, an activity system consists of people, artifacts, an object or motive, sociocultural rules, and roles (Kaptelinin, Nardi, & Macaulav, 1999). Kari Kuutti (1996, p. 27) has characterized *activity* as "a form of doing directed to an object." For these authors an activity is the highest-level objective where the motivations behind the activity and the ultimate objectives or desired outcomes are the same. Within this activity system, multiple actions are performed to reach the overall objective. Each action is driven by a conscious intentional goal. Finally, operations represent unconscious, often routine actions carried

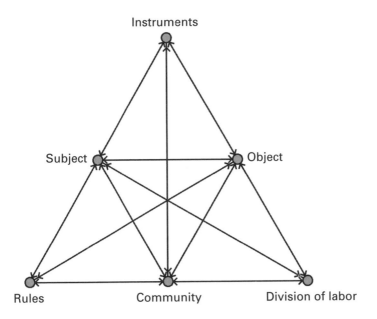

Figure 1.1
Engeström's analysis of activity and mediating relationships

out automatically in the service of other goal-oriented actions. Therefore, the composition of an activity system consists of the activity (the system itself), actions, and operations. Breaking down the system of activity into component parts is useful for identification purposes; however, the system is not reducible to isolated actions or isolated relationships between subjects and tools.

A simple example of the hierarchical structure of activity systems is the activity of "Mark is driving to Aunt Sally's house." The motivation and outcome are for Mark to end up at Aunt Sally's. To realize this outcome, a number of actions might take place: calling Aunt Sally to see when she's available for a visit, checking the weather, printing out driving directions, filling up the car with gas, and so on. On the drive itself, a number of unconscious operations are performed, such as applying the brakes at red lights and using directional signals before changing lanes or making turns. Collectively the motives and actions add up to the final destination. The hierarchy of actions and the identification of the different components of an activity system provide helpful guideposts for articulating and examining the complexity of context. The multilayered nature of activity theory identifies the actions involved in an activity and assesses how these actions relate to each other.

Activity Theory and HCI

The explanatory potential of activity theory lies in the attention that it gives to multiple dimensions of human engagement with the world and in the framework that it provides for configuring those dimensions and processes into a coherent "activity." Critical to understanding these processes of engagement for use in the field of HCI is the mediating role that is played by cultural artifacts or tools and their transformative power. The researchers working at the Human-Computer Interaction Group at Cornell University have focused primarily on mediating devices for communication and learning (figure 1.2). Our research questions have explored how these devices affect outcomes (such as what kind, if any, of communication or learning occurs), process (how does communication or learning occur? what facilitates or inhibits the engagement? who is involved and not involved?), and motivation (how do our notions of communication or learning change? what are our expectations of communication or learning?). Fundamental to the activity theory approach is that humans develop and learn when, in collaboration with others, people act on their immediate surroundings.

Activity theory shares much in common with anthropological, ethnomethodological, and other sociocultural approaches, such as Trevor Pinch and Wiebe Bijker's "The Social Construction of Facts and Artifacts: Or How the Sociology of Science and the Sociology of Technology Might Benefit Each Other" (1987) and Jean Lave and Etienne Wenger's "Legitimate Peripheral Participation in Communities of Practice" (1991). In our work at the HCI Group, we have been drawn to these theories for their common focus on dynamic change, tool mediation, and social construction of meaning. For a more thorough treatment of activity theory history, its recent developments, and its relationship to other sociocultural theories, we refer the reader to a number of excellent sources (e.g., Engeström, 1999a, 1999b, 1999c; Kaptelinin, 1996; Kuutti, 1996; Nardi, 1996a, 1996b). Here we elaborate only on the principles of activity theory that are

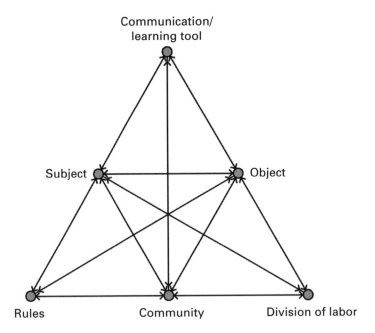

Figure 1.2
Application of Engeström's activity analysis to communication and learning

recurring themes in later chapters—namely, the concepts of mediation, object orientedness, and disturbance.

Mediation

An individual's relationship with and orientation toward an objective is mediated by the tools that are used to attain the objective, the community that participates in the activity, and the division of labor that exists in that community (Engeström, 1999a). In the models of an activity system described above (see figures 1.1 and 1.2), bidirectional arrows indicate multiple mediating relationships within a complex integrated system. Victor Kaptelinin (1996) specifically addresses the mediating effects of computer activity on consciousness, learning, and development. For him, computer technologies have the power to enable and transform activities through the actions, goals, and social relations of individual agents. Our own evaluations of computer mediation confirm these effects, as we describe in later chapters. We emphasize two main insights regarding mediation—the bidirectionality of effects (of the perceptions, motivations, culture, and actions that shape the tool and that are shaped by the tool) and the need for sustained longitudinal studies to reveal how these mediating relationships develop and change over time.

Object Orientedness

In the activity theory model, *object orientedness* (Kaptelinin, 1996, p. 107) refers to humans' engagement with objects (and objectives). Activity theorists ascribe object status to physical, social, and cultural phenomena, including nonmaterial phenomena such as expectations and affinities. The purpose, intent, or motivation of acting on an object or working toward an objective is the foundation of the activity system, and acting on an object is the orienting space of the action.

The HCI Group has identified two important subcategories within the concept of object orientedness: (1) psychological and social objects can be ranked at the same level of importance as physical objects, and (2) artifacts can be transposed into object status and vice versa. An artifact or tool in the primary activity system framework (see figure 1.1), for example, may simultaneously be an object in another system. As a subject interacts with a word-processing program to write a paper, the object is the completed paper, and the artifact or tool is the software program. However, if the program breaks down, the software becomes the object in a new activity of troubleshooting. Likewise, the word-processing program is both a tool for the human subject who uses it and the object of usability research for the designer.

Disturbance

The relationships among the various elements in the activity-theory model are flexible and ever-shifting. In a general account of how activities develop, Yrjo Engeström (1999b) makes the point that activity systems support development and goal attainment but also produce disturbances. In the example of the word-processing program that shifts from being a tool to being an object, this transformation occurs at a breakdown or disturbance. Frank Blacker, Norman Crump, and Seonaidh McDonald (2000) identify other disturbances, such as incoherencies, tensions, and inconsistencies among various components in the system. Engeström (1999b) argues that relationships within activity systems are made orderly only by the determination that people show as they engage with the objects of their activity. As disturbances become evident within and between activity systems, participants may begin to address the underlying issues and change their situations, their activities, or themselves. We have found that disturbances can be informative in the design process as signposts for uncovering why the disturbance materialized, why it did not exist until a given point in time, what the effects of the disturbance might be, and how the disturbance is resolved.

Adding to Activity Theory: An Ecological Perspective

The model of activity theory that is referred to throughout this chapter (that is, the subject, object, and tool relationship) has traditionally been understood as a synchronic, point-in-time depiction of an activity. It does not depict the transformational and developmental processes that provide the focus of much recent activity theory research. In this section, we link activity theory to an ecological perspective to examine another viewpoint and conceptualization of the interplay between systems and the adaptive transformation of systems across time. We are not the first to draw on ecological perspectives for HCI work. Probably the best-known application of this approach is Donald Norman's appropriation of James J. Gibson's (1977, 1979) ecological theory of perception. We turn to ecological theories for two reasons. First, the focus on adaptive systems works well with activity theory and with examining human-computer interaction in context. Second, the ecological metaphor guides our reflection on the evolution and adaptation of our theories and practice of design. Like their biological counterparts, ecologies of ideas (such as activity theory and our application of this theory and related ideas) evolve within complex systems that are novel, are interrelated, and seek to sustain the delicate and necessary balance between the need for stability and the need for change.

In Urie Bronfenbrenner's formulation (1979) of an ecological systems theory of human development, development is a joint function of person and environment. By carefully examining the person within various processes and contexts and asking challenging questions about the nature

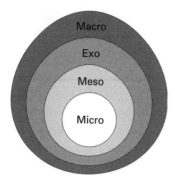

Figure 1.3
Urie Bronfenbrenner's model of an ecological systems theory of human development

of the interaction, researchers can increase the explanatory power of their results. Bronfenbrenner's theory posits an ecology of nested environments or systems—micro, meso, exo, and macro (figure 1.3).

Microsystems, according to Brofenbrenner, consist of "a pattern of activity, roles, and interpersonal relations experienced by the person in a given setting with particular physical and material features and containing other persons with distinctive characteristics of personality and systems of belief" (Bronfenbrenner, 1989, p. 226). Mesosystems "comprise the linkages and process taking place between two or more settings containing the person" (for example, relations between home and school and between school and work) (Bronfenbrenner, 1989, p. 227). Exosystems "encompass the linkage and processes taking place between two or more settings, at least one of which does not ordinarily contain the person, but in which events occur that influence processes within the immediate setting that does not contain the developing person" (for example, for the child, the relation between home and the parent's workplace) (Bronfenbrenner, 1989, p. 227). Macrosystems "consist of the overarching pattern of micro-, meso-, and exosystems characteristic of a given culture, subculture, or other broader social context with particular reference to the developmentally instigative belief systems, resources, life styles, and opportunity structures and patterns of social interchange that are embedded in each of these systems" (Bronfenbrenner, 1989, p. 228). In other words, the macrosystem is the social blueprint for particular cultures, subcultures, or other broader social contexts.

In sum, the micro level of function refers to the individual (plant, animal, and so on) environment and its functions, the meso level refers to interactions of micro environments, the exo level is an outer level that operates indirectly on the environment, and the macro level is the outermost level that defines the global contexts and functions of the system (Engeström, 1999c). Within this ecological model, the issues most relevant for HCI revolve around looking for interaction and interdependence among the levels and the primacy of time and space.

Interaction and Interdependence

Systems do not exist in a vacuum but rather are situated in a broader context of networks of interacting systems. Design questions and practices revolve around the interactions and interdependence of these nested environments. These interactions and their interrelatedness constitute the complexities of design.

Component systems within ecological systems are characterized by progressive, mutual accommodation and extinction throughout the life of the system; these interactions are dynamic processes in and of themselves. As is also true with the principle of disturbance in activity systems, ecological systems are not always harmonious and functioning but have constant tensions, discontinuities, and breakdowns that are necessary for survival and adaptability. The tensions and breakdowns can be used as points of reference for understanding and describing design activity, for example.

Mutual accommodations among system elements shape the relationship among these components, which is interdependent. Changes in any part of a system or among contextual levels have the potential to affect any or all of the other related systems. The developments, tensions, and interrelationships in these systems should be studied in the context of these accommodation processes. As the ecological approach and the process, person, and context model are explored, we describe and account for the transformative power of seemingly ubiquitous artifacts such as language and pervasive computing devices. When an activity system is analyzed at one particular level or context, its relations with activities at other contextual levels (educational systems government, state and local processes) should also be taken into account. This approach reflects what Andrew Pettigrew (1990, p. 269) calls the "importance of embeddedness or studying change in the context of interconnected levels of analysis."

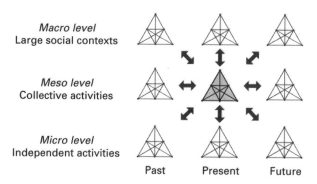

Figure 1.4
Temporal interconnections and "situatedness" of an activity (adapted from Boer, van Baalen, & Kumer, 2002)

Primacy of Time and Space

In addition to the physical network of activity systems, their temporal interconnectedness needs to be examined (Pettigrew, 1990). Activities develop through time, stimulated by the tensions that develop within and between them at various levels (Leont'ev, 1978). "Processes observed at different contextual levels of analysis are often observed to have their own pace and rate" (Boer, van Baalen, & Kumar, 2002, p. 92). Activities from the past are alive in the present and also help shape the future. An activity system is not static, and the developments and changes within the system need to be described and analyzed by locating changes in the past, present, and future (Boer et al., 2002). The dynamic nature of ecological systems hinges on their situatedness in time and space (figure 1.4). Thus, parameters of time and space are the initial critical contexts to which designers need to attend.

Integration of Activity Theory and Ecological Principles

Integrating activity theory with ecological principles involves understanding an outcome (such as a specific technology or user need) at a particular point in time in the context of interacting systems (micro, meso, exo, and macro). The primacy of time and space is particularly crucial because all systems evolve over time and understanding occurs in both historical and contemporary contexts. Activities are "multilevel, multidimensional, dynamic, collective, context-sensitive, and mediated by cultural artifacts" (Boer et al., 2002, p. 8).

The interaction between actors in an activity system is mediated by the object of activity, by language and tools, by a division of labor, by conventions, and by social rules. Participants are involved in a social process as they attempt to accomplish some goal or objective and as they use diverse combinations of signs and tools to create meaning. An activity system can be decomposed into a network of several detailed activity systems—the original setting and increasingly broader contexts (Boer et al., 2002). For example, when analyzing how distributed work teams collaborate on a design project, researchers would look at the history of the work teams and also zoom out to the organizational settings, social settings, and larger social contexts and levels in which these distributed teams operate. The activity system is not only "affected by activity systems at other contextual levels but also exerts influence on them itself. In fact, an activity system can be conceived as a system of distributed cognition" (Boer et al., 2002, p. 6).

The iterative design cycle that is shown in figure 1.5 illustrates the cyclic process of change that is anticipated by activity theory. First, researchers and designers must examine current practices and activities. Needs are identified through scenario-based design techniques, interviews, and observations. Next, tensions, controversies, and conflicts within and between activity systems are identified. Then a period of search and questioning begins as new models and metaphors are considered and new solutions and designs are developed. After the initial series of trials and testing of designs in actual settings, new priorities and approaches emerge, followed by periods of reconceptualization, revision, and redesign. Ultimately, the entire cycle is repeated until some resolution, new stability, or closure is achieved. Increasing agreement among the groups is indicated by a narrowing of disagreements during each iteration, with the resulting central point representing a shared conceptualization or closure (Pinch & Bijker, 1987).

As people begin to address the tensions, conflicts, and breakdowns that are features of their activity systems, they begin to create a collective force for change and innovation (Blacker, Crump, & McDonald, 1999). These breakdowns as well as points of change and development can be used to study activity. The activity-theory approach emphasizes the incoherencies,

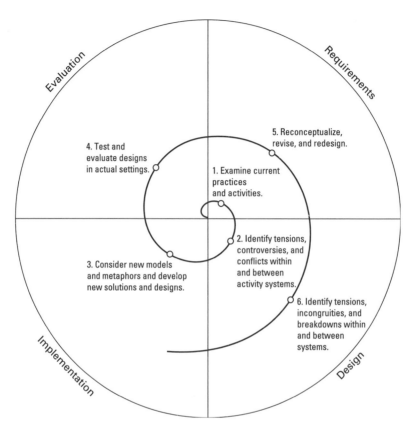

Figure 1.5
An iterative design cycle

tensions, controversies, and conflicts that exist among components in the system (Blacker et al., 1999).

Activities such as technology construction should not be perceived as statically structured entities but rather as dynamic processes that are characterized by ambiguity and change. Construction and renegotiation reoccur constantly within the system. The entire iterative design process rests on dynamic interactions between order and chaos, steady states and breakdowns, harmony and controversy. The activity system is constantly working through tensions within and between its components (Blacker et al., 1999). The tensions and breakdowns that occur within activity sys-

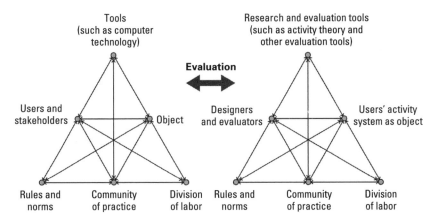

Figure 1.6
The mediating role of evaluation in technology design

tems can be used as points of reference for studying the social construction and design process (Boer et al., 2002).

Within these nested environments are systems that function dynamically and thus enable us to examine how they change over time. Within any design ecology, some systems are perceived as stable and thus require less attention from the designer, while others are perceived as being in flux and become the focus of design research or development. When a new tool is introduced, for example, designers usually focus on user requirements for design (at the micro level), establish these requirements, and then move on to understand the interactions between the new tool and practices in a larger context (meso level).

Toward Reflection in Action

Activity theory cautions us that any tool has the potential to transform the activity in which it is used and, reciprocally, that tools have the potential to be transformed as they are used. Responsible evaluation professionals need to reflect on those potentials and on the ethical considerations that are involved in assessing tool designs, user programs, and evaluation instruments (figure 1.6). Evaluators and designers need to document and analyze uses of technology in program settings and in evaluation activities to understand the mediating functions of different technologies and tools—or, to paraphrase Bonnie Nardi and Vicki O'Day (1999), to engage thoughtfully with technologies as they are used in various contexts.

Evaluation activities are embedded in complex technosystems and cannot be isolated from the system under study. Looking at evaluation as part of the technology design system has transformed how evaluations themselves are designed and conducted (see figure 1.6). In the next few chapters, we describe how we use computer technologies and their multimedia functionalities to collect (multimedia) data, to organize and analyze that data, and to present research findings. These tools can disclose behaviors and social phenomena that have remained hidden and unexamined, even unimagined, because no technologies existed to reveal them. Because new technologies enable new ways of knowing, new ways of evaluating, and new ways of representing and reporting knowledge, they pose methodological, social, and ethical challenges that evaluators need to reflect on and address. Various applications, such as Lotus Notes or concept mapping, can facilitate collaboration among evaluators and stakeholders and offer new ways of conducting evaluations and reflecting on the design process through evaluation activities.

In conclusion, the main contention of this volume is that computer-mediated activity and design need to be understood within their relevant contexts. Activity theory is a holistic approach that can accommodate complexity and diversity by integrating multiple levels of analysis, diverse and multidimensional activities, and various contextual features of computer-mediated communicative practice into a coherent model of human-computer interaction (Nardi, 1996a, 1996b; Engeström, Miettinen, & Punamäki, 1999).

2

Understanding Perspectives: Social Construction of Technology

Introduction

Social interactions play a large role in the development of technology, and they contribute to the inherent ambiguities of technology design (Abowd & Mynatt, 2000; Bødker 1997; Bødker & Petersen 2000; Engeström, 1999a; Hasan, Gould, & Hyland, 1998; Nardi, 1996a, 1996b). The social construction of technology (SCOT) framework considers the multiple social perspectives that surround the development of new technologies (Pinch & Bijker, 1987). SCOT, which evolved out of studies of the sociology of scientific knowledge and the history of technology, examines the multiple "branches" of a technology that coexist to meet the needs of multiple social groups (Edwards, 1995). It explores the ways that individuals, due to their various histories and positions, construct the components and objects of an activity system in different ways.

SCOT theorists describe the social processes that impact technological development and identify the social groups that are responsible for shaping technological artifacts (Bijker & Law, 1992). Fundamentally, as Edwards (1995, p. 212) notes, "technological change is a *social process*: Technologies can and do have 'social impacts,' but they are simultaneously social *products* that embody power relationships and social goals and structures." Like activity theory, SCOT emphasizes multiple social perspectives, social construction, and the use of tools in specified contexts.

A social constructivist approach is ideal for examining the design and development of a technical system (Pinch & Bijker, 1987). Using this approach, the researcher or designer examines the conceptions that are held by the various social groups that are involved in a technology's development and then follows the social construction of each group's technology to examine how the group reaches closure—that is, how that social construction is conceptually frozen in the view of the group and across multiple groups (Pinch & Bijker, 1987). Rather than trying to determine whether the respective conceptions from multiple parties are inherently true or false, the social constructivists situate these conceptions within the context of each group and observe how group members negotiate these conceptions.

The SCOT model encourages designers to consider the interactions, ambiguities, and complexities of the various groups that are defining and developing digital environments and to consider the multiple social perspectives that surround the development of new technologies. This holistic approach contrasts sharply with standard practices in technology development. For example, many designers of computer hardware and software systems tend to isolate the design process from the social and political structure in which they are planned (Kilker & Gay, 1998). Simple measurements of technological performance (such as number of hits on a particular page) are inadequate when isolated from data about the social structure within which the systems are designed or for which they are planned. One of the complex interrelationships among system elements that designers must consider is the impact of various perspectives (Pinch & Bijker, 1987).

A primary assumption of the SCOT approach is that activities are socially co-constructed and mediated by human communication and interaction. Communication and collaboration between subjects are processes that are critical for coordinating different versions of the design and other components of the system. In the early days of networked information, "build it and they will come" may have been a sufficient model of user interest and behavior. Increasingly, however, designers are proactively addressing the particular needs and challenges of their intended users. Ultimately, different versions of a design and various perspectives must be resolved, resulting in consensus or conflict. Through an iterative design process, various stakeholders will reach closure or some agreement (Pinch & Bijker, 1987).

SCOT Concepts

The social construction of technology framework of interpretative flexibility addresses the various notions that are held by each relevant social group. The three main SCOT concepts are relevant social groups, interpretative flexibility, and closure. These concepts—as well as an evaluation of them—are discussed below and further explored in the case study presented later in this chapter.

Relevant Social Groups

Trevor Pinch and Wiebe E. Bijker (1987, p. 30) define *relevant social group* as a group whose members "share a set of meanings attached to a specific artifact." Various relevant social groups can derive very different meanings from a single technology. For example, some of the first SCOT researchers examined the design of early broadcast media and found that relevant social groups' concepts of early radio included radio telegraphy, radio telephony, and broadcasting (Douglas, 1987). Those meanings or interpretations of use create expectations that can lead to alterations in the design of the artifact and to the acceptance of one version of a technology over another. As the radio studies showed, interpretations of the meaning of the proposed technology are shaped by the different disciplinary and organizational cultures to which the project participants belonged.

The multiple actors in a technical development project go through a process of enrolling each other in the enterprise and tailoring the project to meet the different goals of the various actors (Latour, 1987). Relevant social groups differ not only in terms of experience, technical expertise, and goals but also in their ability to influence the final project. The goal and challenge for SCOT theorists is to define the boundaries and relevancy of these social groups.

Interpretive Flexibility

When a technology is first created, it goes through a state that SCOT theorists call *interpretive flexibility,* in which the technological artifact is "culturally constructed and interpreted" as it is being developed and even as it is being used (Pinch & Bijker, 1987, p. 40). Interpretive flexibility describes how different groups perceive a technology and also how these variable perspectives can affect the design and modify the technological artifact. The end product may be very different from the original design or functionality. For example, one of the early conceptions of the use of the telephone was as a radio broadcast medium.

Because design is an ongoing process of interpretation and reshaping, developers benefit from working in tandem with end users and other groups during the planning and production stages. This is especially true when the product or system is without clear or defining boundaries. Pelle Ehn (1988) and others have demonstrated that when developers and users discuss and manipulate a prototype, each group comes to understand multiple perceptions of an emergent technology. These scenarios or prototypes facilitate communication and collaboration processes between groups and help bridge the gap between user needs assessment and the actual design. The challenge is to make these proxies or mockups easily understood by a wide variety of stakeholders.

Closure
User-centered methods often adopt a circular, iterative process in which evaluation is a critical component of a design, build, evaluate, analyze, and redesign spiral (Butler, 1996). After several design iterations—that is, opportunities for developers, evaluators, and users to interact with the technology—the expectation is that the technology will incorporate perspectives of each group (Gay & Bennington, 1999). Gathering information about group expectations and needs can range from qualitative, ethnographic efforts to quantitative methods such as surveys, interviews, and logs. After several iterations, groups eventually share an acceptance or a conceptualization of the technology. The technology is conceptually "frozen" in the view of the groups or stakeholders.

Evaluation
User-centered design techniques emphasize users (Norman, 1998) but, at least in theory, can neglect the many groups and individuals that are involved in the design process. Although user-centered design overturns the old model of "developer knows best" in favor of a new model of "user knows best," in fact, the most productive design exchanges take place

when users, developers, and other groups interact, develop, and maintain a technological innovation.

User-centered methods also fail to identify future uses, needs, and problems that users and developers might not independently envision. This is especially important for nascent technologies, which people will inevitably view in the relatively constrictive terms of old technologies (such as using a digital hand-held machine to replace the old portable audiotape guide system in a museum). Examining the gaps among the views of relevant social groups can identify such issues and ultimately lead to more useful designs.

Our framework for guiding the needs assessment and design of hand-held technologies for museums (see the discussion of Handscape in the case study below) was interpretivism. Consistent with the social construction framework, the philosophical tenets of interpretism focus on deriving meaning and understanding from the varied perspectives of all project participants and relevant social groups. We identified relevant social groups (or stakeholders) and had them state their needs, prioritize them, and critique prototype scenarios. To illustrate this process, we describe a design project called Handscape in the following sections.

The Handscape Study: Using Mobile Technologies to Enhance the Museum Experience

Handscape is an ongoing research project (2001–2004) that has been funded by Intel Corporation and managed by the Human-Computer Interaction Group at Cornell University and by CIMI, an international consortium of museums, application developers, and national standards organizations. To incorporate the perspectives of stakeholder groups into the design of hand-held technologies for museums, we have used the social construction of technology framework to support the needs assessment and design process. The objective of Handscape is to investigate how technology can affect the visitor experience before, during, and after the museum visit. The project evaluators from the HCI Group have examined potential scenarios for mobile computing in museums and tested and evaluated mobile technologies in various museum environments.

Diverse Goals and Concepts

The SCOT approach to design requires stakeholders to be involved early in the process. In the Handscape project, these groups have included the project's funders, museum staff, and administrators, designers, and patrons. Within each group are various subgroups; for example, museum staff includes curators, administrators, and museum educators, and design staff includes programmers, vendors, and interface specialists. Each group has special concerns, goals, and issues.

In our initial needs assessments, we used concept maps to help patrons, designers, and museum professionals understand various perspectives or views of what should be included in a wireless mobile application. Essentially, concept mapping is a process that enables the members of a group or organization to visually depict their ideas on some topic or area of interest. Concept maps have been used to design and develop survey instruments, to construct databases, to begin organizational or project planning, and to analyze research results (Kilker & Gay, 1998; Mead & Gay, 1995). Concept mapping is a "structured process, focused on a topic or construct of interest, involving input from one or more participants, that produces an interpretable pictorial view (concept map) of their ideas and concepts and how these are interrelated" (Trochim, 1985, p. 577). For example, stakeholders can communicate their system preferences electronically via a Web site. Users then can work in the same environment to organize their statements in order of importance. Concept maps are generated using a cluster-analysis technique. All participants can view the statements, list of priorities, and visual maps and gain an understanding of various points of view as well as stated priorities.

Web-Based Concept Mapping

In the initial phase of the Handscape project, approximately 115 people participated in the statement-generation stage, and responses were collected from thirty-five museum professionals, eighteen system designers and vendors, and sixty-two museum patrons. Museum professionals included science writers, directors of education and digital media, chief curators, vice presidents, and information officers.

Because the initial stage of the process was Internet-based, participants could complete this task from remote locations. Participants were directed to a Web page that presented several possible scenarios involving wireless, mobile computing applications in museums. At the Web page, they read the examples, viewed scenario-based images as a stimulus, and then were automatically directed to a statement-generation Web page that consisted of a *focus prompt* (a statement used to guide the statement-generation process) followed by a list of previously submitted statements. The goal was to generate an exhaustive list of ideas about the integration of mobile technologies into museums.

Participants in the statement-generation stage were given the opportunity to add to the statement list freely. Statements were subsequently used in the next two phases of the project. An important benefit of using participants' actual statements is that the emergent conceptual framework is entirely in the language of the participants, which is consistent with the objectives of SCOT. In all, 110 unique statements were generated.

The next phase of the project required participants from the three stakeholder groups—museum professionals, designers and vendors, and patrons—to complete a sorting task in which they grouped all generated statements into conceptually similar groups and labelled each group. In summary, participants from each group brainstormed a list of 110 statements relating to wireless computing applications in museums and then sorted and rated the statements. The resulting semantic similarities in statements and their priority rankings allowed us to compare characteristics of expectations among stakeholder groups. Together, these analyses produced the cluster diagram presented in figure 2.1.

The bottom and the lower left of the cluster map (see figure 2.1) contains two related concepts—location and administration. The location category involves providing users with directions to a help desk, emergency exits, and specific exhibits. It also includes the idea of museum floor plans that show users their location and the location of the exhibits they have previously visited. The location cluster statements focus on user end functionality as it relates to way-finding applications. Since enough statements relating to way finding were generated, participants grouped these ideas together often enough to warrant a distinct group. The administration

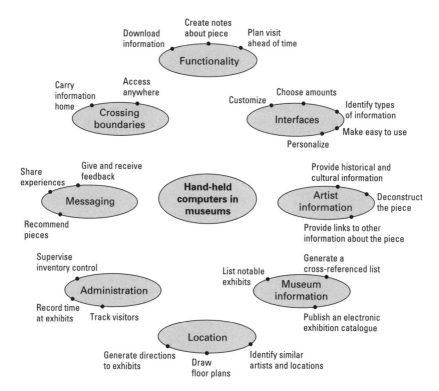

Figure 2.1
The first stage of the Handscape project: Statement generation (a cluster map)

category addresses the business end of museum operations, such as promoting gift shop sales, monitoring the popularity of exhibits, and tracking users' behavior during their visits.

The content-related clusters are artist information and museum information. Artist information encompasses historical, cultural, and chronological information, including statements about an artist's other works and exhibits, the creation process of the pieces, and any restoration work completed. Museum information includes the displays, statistics about the museum, and an electronic exhibition catalog.

In figure 2.1, the artist information and museum information categories are located directly across from the messaging cluster, which contains statements focusing on the social and interactional potential of wireless technology. People envisioned mobile devices as pushing information to

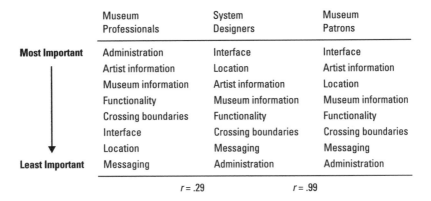

	Museum Professionals	System Designers	Museum Patrons
Most Important	Administration	Interface	Interface
	Artist information	Location	Artist information
	Museum information	Artist information	Location
	Functionality	Museum information	Museum information
	Crossing boundaries	Functionality	Functionality
	Interface	Crossing boundaries	Crossing boundaries
	Location	Messaging	Messaging
Least Important	Messaging	Administration	Administration
		$r = .29$	$r = .99$

Figure 2.2
Stakeholder rankings of eight objectives for enhancing the museum experience with technology

users but did not see the potential for using the devices for two-way communication and interaction.

Finally, in the crossing-boundaries cluster, patrons express their desire to extend their visitor learning experiences beyond the walls of the museum. These statements highlight the potential for patrons to download and bring information home with them—through the development of automated, seamless systems that electronically send relevant information to visitors on completion of their visit to a museum, for example.

Figure 2.2 shows how the three stakeholders—museum professionals, system designers, and museum patrons—ranked eight objectives for enhancing the museum experience with mobile technologies. Clearly, these groups had different priorities. A high correlation was found between the rankings done by the designers and patrons ($r = .99$), and a much lower correlation was found between the rankings done by these groups and by museum professionals ($r = .29$). Designers and patrons were concerned with basic features of the hand-held technologies, such as visual, auditory, downloading, and visit-planning capabilities. These groups were also concerned about screen size, flexibility, and usability. Both the patrons and system designers felt that location- and way-finding features should be included in a wireless application. On the other hand, museum staff and administrators were most concerned with pushing the content, such as information about artists, paintings, and the physical museum.

For all stakeholders, messaging—which would allow users to view and provide feedback on art, make recommendations about particular exhibits, annotate pieces, and interact with museum curators and staff—was consistently rated as less important than the other categories in this initial needs assessment. Despite the view of many people that a visit to the museum is a social experience, messaging and opportunities to interact with the exhibits were ranked low (Gay & Stefanone, 2002).

In summary, these ranking results inform several dimensions of integrating wireless mobile computing applications in museum contexts across three relevant social groups. The responses of the stakeholders reveal insights into some pressing questions concerning the ways that museum visitors might utilize mobile computing applications. Aside from offering museum patrons access to content that relates to museum exhibits, the proposed technology would also offer them messaging capabilities and way-finding applications that cross the traditional physical boundaries of museums.

Nevertheless, in this initial needs assessment, stakeholders ranked the messaging or social aspect of wireless technology lower in importance than the content traditionally developed by museums, such as information about artists, artworks, and the museum itself. Many of the museum professionals and patrons saw mobile technologies as simply upgraded digital audio guides and electronic information cards.

Perceptions after Testing Prototypes

In the second phase of the needs assessment, we asked museum professionals who had tested mobile computing prototypes to sort the statements generated by the three stakeholder groups in the first phase. Museum professionals from the Field Museum in Chicago, the American Museum of the Moving Image (AMMI) in New York, and Kew Gardens, London, participated in the second mapping exercise (figure 2.3). Comparing this figure with figure 2.2 reveals some interesting findings. Whereas the museum professionals in figure 2.2 consistently rated administration (including using hand-helds to organize and maintain collections) as their most important objective for the technology, museum professionals who had experience with implementing hand-held devices rated administration as or near least important. Messaging, on the other hand, moved from the

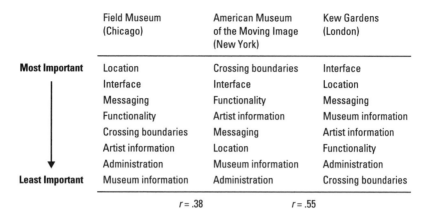

	Field Museum (Chicago)	American Museum of the Moving Image (New York)	Kew Gardens (London)
Most Important	Location	Crossing boundaries	Interface
	Interface	Interface	Location
	Messaging	Functionality	Messaging
	Functionality	Artist information	Museum information
	Crossing boundaries	Messaging	Artist information
	Artist information	Location	Functionality
	Administration	Museum information	Administration
Least Important	Museum information	Administration	Crossing boundaries
		$r = .38$	$r = .55$

Figure 2.3
Museum professional rankings of the initial stakeholders' rankings of eight objectives for enhancing the museum experience with technology

lowest ranking to a significantly higher rating of importance after museum professionals tested the devices with actual visitors (Gay & Stefanone, 2002).

Given the different contexts of the three museums involved in the rankings shown in figure 2.3, a high level of variability was expected among ratings, but many rankings are consistent across all three museums. Issues relating to the interface of hand-held systems (including usability, flexibility, and uncluttered screen design) ranked highest in perceived importance among the three institutions.

Finally, at follow-up interviews with participants at the three museums, users in these settings reported that they were interested in devices that could promote social interactions with museum visitors and staff. For example, several people mentioned that museums should try to include recommender systems (organized recommendation-sharing programs), annotation features, and ways to communicate with others. Young users mentioned a feature that would allow visitors to meet one another and possibly tour the museum together.

Many of the museum professionals expressed concerns that mobile technologies that incorporate video and audio would interfere with the museum experience—that people would attend to their computing devices rather than to the objects in the museum. Museum professionals also worried about access, control, and cost issues.

Setting Priorities

The statement-generating concept map (see figure 2.1), the stakeholders' rankings of objectives for the hand-held technologies (see figure 2.2), and the museum professionals' assessments posttesting (see figure 2.3) helped stakeholders to understand their own goals and objectives and their priorities compared to other groups' concerns. Museum personnel and designers realized that they needed to address some of the concerns of patrons sooner rather than later in the project.

Several groups had markedly different concerns about hand-held technology design and use, ranging from using hand-held technologies for managing collections and audiences to attracting young people to museums. One benefit of interpretive flexibility is that designers examine stakeholders' concerns, consider the preferences of users with different perspectives, and evaluate the extent that various stakeholders' preferences should be incorporated into the new system. The comments made on surveys and in concept-mapping sessions served as a catalyst for renegotiating the museum's goals, specifications, and solutions. Participants in this study, for example, are beginning to focus on designing technologies for young people and audiences who do not traditionally visit museums. Museums are also beginning to examine the issue of integrating communication and messaging tools into the prototypes—something that they did not originally cite as a priority.

Our original evaluation goal for this study was to understand the features that should be included in a single mobile computing application to satisfy a broad range of museum interests. We have found it difficult to find closure for any particular idea or set of ideas for museum applications. Wireless technology standards are constantly changing, and people are becoming accustomed to using mobile devices for a number of activities, including phoning friends, accessing and managing schedules, accessing the Web, and mapping geographical routes.

Because of the ubiquitous and flexible nature of these small mobile appliances, the need to create specific museum applications suited for one or two audiences may no longer be necessary. Designers can incorporate several customizable designs based on the preferences expressed in the evaluation results of relevant social groups (see chapter 5).

Finally, evaluators need to use various methods to discover discrepancies early in the design process and communicate these discrepancies to relevant groups. If discrepancies are not uncovered, development could continue based on incorrect or incomplete visions of the needs of end-users and other stakeholders (Kilker & Gay, 1998).

A Social Constructivist Approach to Design and Evaluation

As with any useful analytical approach SCOT's ultimate benefit lies in its ability to help researchers reframe the problem under study and to help designers understand the goals of important stakeholders (Kilker & Gay, 1998). This approach emphasizes the importance of social interactions in the design of technology, uses an interpretive framework to understand inconsistent results, resists premature closure of the design process, considers the ways that relevant social groups are mediated and their differing levels of influence on technology, and approaches iterative design and evaluation as a socially constructed and negotiable process.

We found that our primary function as evaluators was to promote communication among the relevant social groups participating in the design process and to help those groups understand the differing needs of all the stakeholders in the process. Evaluators can serve as closure mechanisms by acting as intermediaries between the users and other relevant groups involved in design. As demonstrated by the Handscape needs analysis, the shortcomings of traditional evaluation models can be overcome by adopting a group-centered design for collecting, analyzing, and reporting evaluation data.

The relevancy of a social group to a technology is not static but can change over the course of a project. For example, the influence of museum patrons on hand-held technology design can increase as systems are installed and tested, as evidenced in the museum case study presented in this chapter. Groups can also render themselves more (or less) relevant by participating in (or opting out of) the design process. Stakeholders' beliefs about design, interactivity, and the museum experience itself have shaped both the design process and final product.

The technology reflects what the relevant stakeholders (museum professionals, system designers, and museum patrons) believe is useful, appropriate, and, in fact, possible, and the design process is one of constant negotiation among group members with different backgrounds, strengths, and goals. While museum patrons might prefer to see more user participation in the design of software for mobile technology devices, museum professionals might be reluctant to involve others in decisions about how the museum presents itself. Programmers and designers might see technical challenges and opportunities but neglect to take into account complex political and economic issues.

A challenge with implementing a framework that employs a social construction of technology framework is to define the boundaries and roles of different social groups. To be relevant, a SCOT framework must balance the needs of the various groups that are involved in design and evaluation and their various notions of the actual and desirable levels of influence that each group holds. During any evaluation process, evaluators should examine why certain groups are more or less influential and what consequences these influences have over the course of a project. Evaluators can help interpret the demands of different groups, help each group understand the perspective of other groups, depoliticize technology development, and help groups reach consensus or closure (Kilker & Gay, 1998).

Conclusion

An interpretivist approach, such as the SCOT framework that is advanced in this chapter, takes a contextually based perspective that values the multiple understandings, intentions, involvement, and perspectives of all project participants. This approach orients interpretivist inquiry within a meaningful framework that facilitates the evaluation processes, illuminates tacit assumptions and contextual issues, and enhances the trustworthiness and credibility of the findings by grounding them in users' understandings.

Design is situated in a network of influencing social systems, and building any technological system is a socially constructed and negotiable process. By using an interpretive flexibility framework, developers can understand stakeholders' various goals and apparent inconsistencies. When using the SCOT model, researchers are required to highlight differing perceptions of a technology, gather differing assessments of the technology's performance, determine the features that should be incorporated, and decide the way that the features should operate in any given context. The goals of the various groups involved in the production of a technology can be very different, and therefore their interpretations of the project tend to differ as well.

In conclusion, the design of any technical system requires careful consideration of the interactions among the various groups that are working to define and develop the system. To design an effective system that meets the needs of various users, consistent and simultaneous attention must be paid to a variety of social, organizational, administrative, and technical concerns (Kilker & Gay, 1998; Levy & Marshall, 1995). The SCOT framework offers an important approach to this potentially daunting challenge.

3

Creating a Sense of Place: Designing for Online Learning Conversations

Introduction

For several years, we have been experimenting with knowledge-sharing tools to enhance learning conversations in collaborative virtual environments (CVEs). CVEs are online areas where people can communicate and interact with each other in a number of ways by using text, video, sound, avatars, multiuser domains (MUDS), or other combinations of virtual contact. CVEs allow participants in different places to occupy a virtual space and have a common frame of reference for collaborative activity.

In this chapter, we examine reactions to tools that allow users to discuss and view art objects online. As researchers, we were interested in designing and testing virtual spaces that facilitate online conversations by providing social cues and easy ways to interact with others. The way in which these CVEs are designed and operate affect the ways that we communicate and employ social conventions. We do know that people have difficulty using virtual reality and other complex systems (Erickson, Halverson, Kellogg, Laff, & Wolf, 2002). Despite the many research studies that have been conducted and the many technological innovations for supporting mediated conversations that have been made, researchers continue to be uncertain of what works and what does not work in CVE design.

Designing Systems for Conversing: A Research Setting

Face-to-face situations are flexible and dynamic and provide rich contextual cues—facial expressions, vocal tones, and body postures and gestures—that help people interpret and conduct conversations (Goffman, 1959). These cues enable speakers to frame their interactions appropriately and understand what is happening in a particular context or situation (Goffman, 1974). Many of the signals that inform senders that a channel is open or that reception is taking place are missing in online environments. In fact, before we can conceive of a virtual environment or an online conversation space, we need to develop an understanding of face-to-face activities and practices in particular spaces (e.g., Clark & Brennan, 1991).

When people view art through a prototypical museum Web site, they lose the social aspect of viewing and discussing images in the museum or other social setting. Experiencing the collection becomes a solitary activity that provides online viewers with no opportunity to talk about their impressions with others, to watch others interact, or simply to walk with others. In our studies, we were interested in incorporating social cues or structures that would be useful in supporting conversations. To this end, we built a simple system that would make it easy to initiate, conduct, or share conversations about an object with another individual or with a small group of people. In our design prototypes, we examined aspects of museum settings, the use of sources of information, affordances (possibilities for action), appropriation, issues of authority and trust, and conventions for online conversations.

Learning Conversations

Learning is built up through conversations between persons or among groups and involves the creation of shared understanding through social interactions (Schegloff, 1991; Schegloff & Sacks, 1973). These conversations are the means by which people collaboratively construct beliefs and meanings and state their differences. Common ground or mutual knowledge is established and negotiated through successive turns of action and talk (Clark & Brennan, 1991; Goodwin & Heritage, 1986; Schegloff, 1991). Harold Garfinkel (1967), Garfinkel and Harvey Sacks (1970), Hugh Mehan and Houston Wood (1975), and Emanuel A. Schegloff and Sacks (1973) have highlighted the importance of using the resources of the physical world to establish a common or socially shared meaning. For example, people can be drawn into a conversation about an object, and the object, in turn, provides a focal point to support the discussion. Images can help focus and maintain attention (Nardi et al., 1993; Suchman, 1987). When people talk, they continuously represent and refer to objects or things to help them achieve some level of common ground or understanding.

Designing systems that improve communication and understanding must consider the purpose of a conversation in a given situation and the process by which the conversation unfolds. Conversation is first a source of data; the information communicated between participants in a conversation provides the raw data with which people construct knowledge and understanding and enter into a community of practice. The process of conversation also helps people learn such critical skills as how to talk about ideas, how to analyze and discuss ideas with others, and how to present information to others.

Face-to-face conversation also allows for timely feedback by the listener. In general, a listener in a conversation provides the speaker with positive evidence ("uh huh," "yeah," and so on) or negative evidence ("pardon?," quizzical facial expressions, and so on) of comprehension, depending on whether the listener believes that he or she has understood what the speaker means (Clark, 1996). Students, for example, continuously provide their instructors with evidence of their understanding of given concepts. Instructors can monitor this type of evidence in face-to-face conversations and use it to adjust their communication.

Through conversations, experienced persons in a field pass along their knowledge to others by telling stories, answering questions, and discussing information (Garfinkel & Sacks, 1970). Therefore, one major issue that faces designers of systems to support learning conversations concerns helping one person or group understand others and create and maintain common ground.

In the next section, we describe several museum ecologies or distinctive sets of visitor experiences. By finding out why people visit museums and what they do during these visits, designers can use these observations to guide the designs of online spaces to support social interactions.

Museum Ecologies: An Overview

Museum researchers have identified three primary museum ecologies to describe the visitor experience—the sacred-space ecology, the social and recreational ecology, and the learning ecology. Each of these ecologies describes a distinctive set of experiences for visitors (Bell, 1999). In other words, visitors at museums can encounter things that uplift the mind and spirit, take them away from the everyday and routine, and allow them to encounter and discriminate beauty; they can have fun and interact and participate with others; and they can learn something, celebrate great events and people, and connect with the past.

The sacred-space ecology was originally described by Ian Hamilton Finlay (1977), who argued that many visitors use the museum as an escape from the outside world, similar to the way that some people use a church to find solace. Hilde S. Hein (2000) agrees, writing that some people view a museum as a secular temple and feel awe at being in the presence of culturally significant items. The ideal museum visit should allow the visitor the opportunity to experience luminality, a passage of time set apart from the rest of life that provides a transformative, spiritual, and moving experience (Bell, 1999). Neil G. Kotler and Philip Kotler (1998) observe that "great museum exhibitions offer visitors transcendent experiences that take them outside the routines of everyday life and transport them into new and wonderful worlds of beauty, thought, and remembrance." Colette Dufresne-Tassé (1995) argues that the most obvious benefit of a museum visit is experiencing various pleasures, including the pleasures derived from observing beautiful or important objects, coming in contact with something new, and identifying with the beautiful.

Another important museum ecology is a social one. Selma Thomas (1998) defines an exhibition as a conversation between the museum and its audience. Regardless of the type of museum, patrons often like to visit museums with other people or groups—as part of a couple, family, class, or group of friends. "Museum spaces, while seemingly imposing and alienating, have been appropriated by visitors as large public spaces in which to engage in social activities. The visit-ritual element here is about socializing with other museum visitors" (Bell, 1999, p. 3).

The final museum ecology is that of learning. People go to museums to be educated about something—to learn about a particular period of history, person, or work of art (Bell, 1999). Hein (2000) has suggested that museums should be a place to learn how to interpret and understand these objects from various perspectives. In a similar vein, David Carr (1999, p. 35) has argued that "if it is to make human insights possible, the museum needs to help its users become insightful and to embrace sensation as well as cognition at learning's heart." The museum should facilitate a learning process that empowers visitors to make better-informed judgments and decisions long after they leave the museum building (Kenne, 1998; Well, 1990).

Perhaps no single museum ecology is more important than another, and the experiences that these three ecologies describe are not necessarily mutually exclusive. Even so, finding a balance among them can be difficult.

Tensions, Constraints, and Barriers

Although identifying these separate dimensions of the museum experience is a fairly straightforward analytical task, finding a balance among these experiences can be difficult. Kristine Morrissey and Douglas Worts (1998) write that the museum has played two often conflicting roles in society. One role is that of a temple—a sacred space where objects, mystery, authority, and rituals lead museum patrons to make a connection with the spiritual realm. The other role is that of a forum—a neutral space where museum patrons can share ideas, activities, memories, dreams, and questions and can argue their positions. Museums have fulfilled these roles only partially, and they rarely fulfill both roles at the same time.

In addition, a tension exists between enjoying art for aesthetic purposes and learning from art. Focusing too heavily on education risks ruining the pleasure that can be derived from viewing beautiful works (Bell, 1999). Similarly, a tension exists between the learning and social aspects of the museum visit. Reading large amounts of text, for instance, is incompatible with being social (Mintz, 1998).

An especially challenging conflict arises between the view that museums should be an outlet for community values and the view that museums should maintain objectivity to avoid offending or disrespecting any person or group (Evans, 1995). However, museums, by their nature, have values. Even when a museum is trying to be objective in an exhibit, it might insult some people by the information that it presents. People can disagree about the meaning of almost every experience. To some, for instance, learning means understanding the message that the museum is trying to communicate; to others, it means using surroundings to come to conclusions about the world, society, and the self (Bell, 1999; Hein, 2000).

Museums also operate within various kinds of constraints. Some constraints are perceptual and cultural: "Many potential visitors feel intimidated by the aura of 'elite' knowledge they perceive museums to embody. They feel that they don't know enough to go to a museum" (Bell, 1999, p. 4). Others perceive museums as boring and uninteresting.

In addition to these perceptual and cultural constraints, some constraints flow from the museum's goals for the visitor experience. For example, museum professionals strive for the museum experience to be visitor oriented and try to design exhibits that take into account visitor needs in the available space. Museums also try to provide a variety of information, build facilities that speak to the needs of visitors, and account for the knowledge, perceptions, and attitudes that visitors bring with them to a learning situation (Hooper-Greenhill, 2000).

To ameliorate some of these constraints and simultaneously address the diverse needs and goals of visitors, museums are turning to new information technologies to bring their collections to a wider public. In general, the population is sophisticated about media culture and experienced in digital interactive technology. In particular, the popularity of digital games and media culture in general suggests that young museum patrons need to be entertained and engaged. Some hints about how technology might help designers overcome constraints on the museum experience come from visitors' expectations of online sites. For example, visitors to online sites expect high-quality images, customization capabilities, in-depth information about objects, and access to other visitors or to museum personnel for information (Sugita, Hong, Reeve, & Gay, 2002).

Because the designers of current museum online spaces assumed that the computer is primarily a tool for disseminating predefined information, they have failed to overcome the constraints on maximizing the museum experience that are outlined above. Viewing a collection online becomes a solitary activity, and viewers have no opportunities to discuss with others their interpretations and impressions of the works on display, despite the fact that most people learn about art, artifacts, and images by discussing them.

The ArtView Study: Spatial Metaphors and Conversational Props

The intent of the ArtView program that we developed was to provide students, teachers, and professionals at remote sites with a shared, virtual information and discussion space where they could discuss and analyze objects and artifacts. ArtView enables students and researchers who cannot travel to a museum or library to experience the institution's collection and to discuss works with others.

In this section, we provide a distillation of the experiences of students and facilitators who used ArtView (Gay, Boehner, & Panella, 1997). Even though we have been involved in several computer-mediated communication (CMC) design projects over the years (Gay & Lentini, 1995; Gay, Sturgill, Martin, & Huttenlocher, 1999), this case study illustrates and illuminates a number of the issues that are involved in designing and employing collaborative virtual environments. In one year, the Human-Computer Interaction Group at Cornell built and tested several versions of ArtView and other CVE applications. Art history, psychology, and communication students used ArtView, created archived chats, and provided additional feedback to designers and museum personnel through interviews. Students compared their experiences in a face-to-face guided museum visit with their experiences in a computer-mediated viewing and discussion using ArtView. For this analysis, we drew primarily on observations, chat log files, and interviews using qualitative data-analysis techniques.

ArtView is a two-dimensional space that uses a museum metaphor of moving from exhibit to exhibit with a group of people. Each exhibit, painting, or artifact serves as a focal point for online discussions. Students were presented with a selector screen (called "The Museum") that contained thumbnail images of objects from the collection, the title of the image, and the number of "visitors" who were currently viewing each of the images (figure 3.1).

Figure 3.1
ArtView's selection screen

After an image or a viewing space was selected, the screen refreshed to show an enlarged view of the image, a chat window, the name of the person sharing the "room," and a series of selection buttons (figure 3.2). All the students who were looking at an image online could communicate in real time via the chat window. The idea was to replicate the experience of visiting a museum, walking up to a painting or artifact, and discussing the object with the other people who were standing in the same space. When a student was ready to discuss an object with others, he or she clicked on "Join Group" and invited others to join him or her in the "room." The inviter acted as a group leader and controlled the images that the group viewed and the length of time that the image was displayed. When forming the group, the leader could choose to designate the group as "private." Members of a private group saw only comments made by other members of their group; the comments of people who were viewing the same picture

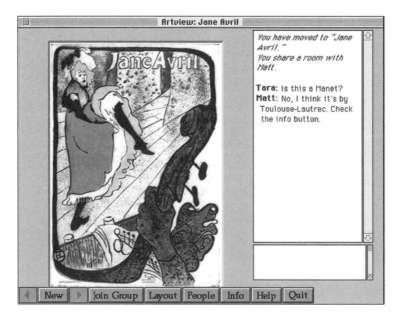

Figure 3.2
ArtView's enlarged view of an image and a chat window

but who were not members of the private group were not displayed to the group members. This private-group feature enabled curators, artists, and educators to take visitors on "tours" of the collections without interference from other visitors (figure 3.3).

In a later version of ArtView, we used three-dimensional spaces to replicate the experience of walking up to a painting and using visual cues to determine the number of people who were viewing objects in a particular area (figure 3.4). In this version, students could make full-bodied avatars walk through museum spaces by using the computer mouse or arrow keys. Users could personalize or customize their avatars and move around exhibits with others or by themselves. Visitors in the three-dimensional space communicated via the chat window.

When participants in an online study conduct online conversations, they generate a record that helps researchers gain an understanding of how a particular tool was used by participants. A rich description of activities, specific patterns of use, and attitudes can be identified when these online tracking systems are triangulated with other data, such as focus-group

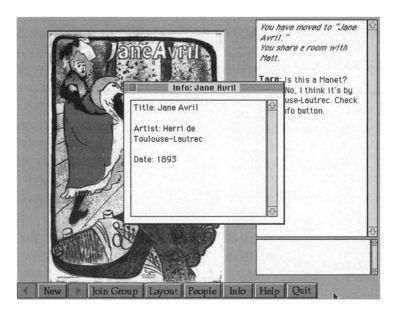

Figure 3.3
ArtView's private-group feature: a text box displayed only to group members

sessions, surveys, observation, and video and audio taping. Using these techniques, we paid particular attention to the affective dimensions of the user experience in these sessions.

In the next sections, we briefly describe use activities and reactions to these conversation spaces. Finally, we highlight some of the themes that emerged from these studies.

Replicating the Museum's Role as Social Place

The museum provides an experience of artworks with an accompanying ambiance. ArtView tries to combine the artworks and the ambiance by providing users with access to art reproductions, information about the art, and communication about the art with other people. The communication channel was designed to invoke some of the social atmosphere of a museum.

Many participants in this study stressed that the museum's role as a social place was, in fact, an important aspect of their art-viewing experience. Most said that they usually went to museums with friends or family mem-

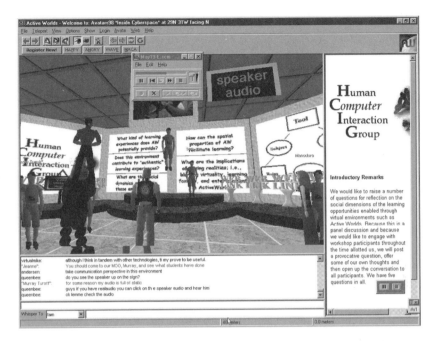

Figure 3.4
ArtView's three-dimensional avatar space

bers and that the opportunity to discuss works was key to a satisfying visit. Participants appreciated that ArtView introduced this communication space for dialogue and analysis into the online environment. For this reason, they rated ArtView favorably compared to their experiences with other museum Web sites. Traditional museum Web sites were primarily information resources, whereas ArtView created a space for real-time communication. The participants ultimately concluded that ArtView, museum Web sites, and actual museum visits should be complementary rather than competing applications for experiencing art:

> *Karen:* ArtView definitely has a more classroom, discussion-type, feel to it. The focus is more on talking about the art than simply getting info on a certain piece. Museum Web sites are not as interactive. . . . The information is more static. In ArtView, the available info depends mostly on the people and how involved they get.

Participants stated that ArtView's ability to support real-time conversations about a given object or set of objects provided a dynamic, interactive way of viewing art online. A museum also supports this function, but participants commented that they did not always have a partner with whom to converse and sometimes felt that conversation was discouraged. In ArtView, participants indicated that they felt comfortable discussing the different pieces. This feeling of comfort was described on two levels—as a level of competence in participating in a conversation about art and as a level of satisfaction in the conversation itself.

The open-ended nature of the conversation also meant that many people could participate in a discussion simultaneously. As has been shown in other studies of electronic support for group discussion (Dennis, George, Jessup, Nunamaker, & Vogel, 1988), when everyone has equal access to the chat space, no one person can completely dominate the discussion. Everyone in a particular ArtView session or group space had the chance to express an opinion, ask a question, or redirect the conversation. The informal atmosphere of ArtView appeared to provide a comfortable forum for expression. Additionally, although people reported that they were often intimidated by museums, the relative anonymity of ArtView allowed them to feel less inhibited, which may have increased participation. One participant claimed that being anonymous allowed her to feel more comfortable participating in the ArtView discussion than in a discussion at the physical museum:

> *Jennifer:* ArtView seems to be a better medium for *discussing* art. I don't feel nearly as comfortable speaking in public as I do typing, where I am physically hidden.

In terms of recreating the social and learning ecologies of museums, ArtView was a qualified success. The technologies also provided some losses, however, which our research sought to identify.

Lack of Social Conventions and Cues

As positive as most participants were about the opportunity to communicate with others, they also identified some of the difficulties of communicating online in real time solely through text. In text-based conversations, people cannot use the physical and vocal cues and "turn-taking" behaviors that help to regulate group discussion in face-to-face situations (Hancock & Dunham, 2001). The lack of social conventions and of cues that signal when and where to contribute often leads to confusion. For example, during online sessions, several participants can type and enter comments simultaneously. As a result, the pace of dialogue can be very fast. Because it is not always clear who is responding to whom, group discussions can quickly fragment into multiple threads of conversation (Black, Levin, Mehan, & Quinn, 1983; Gay, Boehner, & Panella, 1997). This "disruption of conversational adjacency"—presenting ideas out of order and violating the socially learned rules of conversational responses—makes it difficult to interpret messages and to synchronize actions among participants (e.g., Herring, 1999). An atmosphere of ambiguity can emerge in the group relationship. Lack of immediate feedback can disturb the synchronicity of the communication flow among group members, and often little or no explicit acknowledgment is made that messages have been received. When participants are not sure whether unacknowledged messages are being ignored by choice or being passed over inadvertently, communication is inefficient and even misinterpreted. Although participants in Internet chat spaces tend to learn to adapt to these problems, participants in the ArtView study felt ignored and lost track of conversations:

> *Anne:* I sometimes felt that I wouldn't be able to get my opinion in where I wanted it before the topics we were discussing completely changed.

Also, because contributions to ArtView conversations were simultaneous rather than sequential, the text on the screen multiplied quickly. People typed in a question or comment and then waited for a response. After a brief pause, four or five replies appeared, and others tried to respond to all of them. Several people felt that it was difficult to determine when to move to the next picture. Without facial or physical cues to read, the periods of inactivity were difficult to interpret. Silence could mean that the respondent was busy typing, had nothing to say, needed help, or wanted to move to the next piece or room.

Others indicated that for educational purposes, for example, more social conventions would be needed. For the students, the relative lack of social conventions and norms that govern face-to-face conversations, such as turn taking and gestural cues, resulted in confusion about when and whether to contribute. One person pointed out the high probability for confusion:

> *Craig:* I would be responding to one person, and four or five other people would add something. It all happened really fast, so it was difficult to follow what was happening.

The addition of three-dimensional avatars and more realistic space did not seem to resolve the issues of turn taking and simultaneous communication. Even though participants could choose an avatar and move through the virtual museum space, conversation with others was limited to a text-based chat box. Participants also became distracted when they moved their avatars through space and spent more time dealing with the distractions of negotiating through space than conversing with others. People complained that the avatars disrupted conversations:

> *Lynn:* It was too hard trying to type and move my avatar around. By the time I got my avatar to a particular painting, I forgot what we were supposed to be talking about.

Finally, while the informal quality of online discussion may encourage participation, it can also relax participants' academic focus. When we analyzed the chat logs, we discovered that many people made one or two contributions to the discussion and then began to make irrelevant or irreverent comments. In both the two-dimensional and three-dimensional applications of ArtView, most participants said that they were satisfied with the quality of conversations even though the researchers felt that many of the discussions lost focus and direction. The participants held mixed views on whether the physical museum or the online discussion was more satisfying. Students who argued in favor of the real museum experience indicated that in-person conversations were more thorough and less disjointed:

> *Andy:* Questions were asked and thoroughly explored *[in the face-to-face discussions]*. It was a lot more enlightening as far as the depth and quality of the conversation goes. It is always easier for a group to converse in person than on a computer.

Overall, these participants felt that the discussions in the museum were more productive and easier to follow. The museum experience provided more visual and aural cues than the online spaces, and the docents in the museum space guided discussions about pieces and kept the visit focused. The ArtView conversations tended to be repetitive and digressed quickly to topics other than the picture under observation.

Authority

Participants were also concerned about the role that was played by the facilitator in the ArtView online environment. Situations in which the authorities or docents actively guided discussions—whether online or in the museum—were the most satisfying. However, in a text-based environment, people felt that museum experts or teachers lost some of their identifiability and hence their status. Since the online environment offered no proxemic or appearance cues, the authorities' comments were represented just like everyone else's.

Visitors to the site said that they were somewhat discomforted by this blurring of status roles. Coupled with the difficulties of text-based communication cited above, the visitors also felt that the expert's loss of status cues caused the online discussions to be generally less focused than face-to-face discussions were. Participants suggested that discussion leaders' comments should be displayed in bold or in a different color from the surrounding text to provide them with greater "visual authority" and to distinguish their comments from those of the students. Others suggested that experts could help keep people focused by providing discussion questions and other interesting bits of information:

> *Susan:* I got the feeling that the discussions in the museum were much more directed than the discussions on ArtView because I think the person leading the discussion loses a lot of their authority when their voice is the same text as everybody else's. It makes the leader of the group just another member of the group.

After analyzing the chat logs, we found that students made one or two serious comments and then rapidly started making irrelevant comments about the objects. Because the irrelevant and inaccurate statements were mixed in with the serious comments, people were worried about the credibility of the information from others online and the trustworthiness of the sources of the information.

As a result of the students' suggestions in the first ArtView tests, we added more visible facilitators to the online discussions for the second round of testing. This attempt to guide and organize the sessions also changed the dynamics of the sessions. Most users acknowledged that the structured online discussions were more thorough and more in line with what they expected to hear in a conversation about art. The museum professionals or facilitators provided information, and the ensuing discussion revolved around deconstructing a piece of art. After the structured sessions, students complained that they would rather have a distribution of authority and more opportunities for informal discussions. Several students felt threatened or inhibited during the structured sessions:

> *Jan:* I hesitated to participate in the discussions because I was worried that people would think I was stupid.

Groups using collaborative virtual environments may be obligated to reassess the relationship between providing leadership and ensuring that every group member has an equal voice in the process. Computer-mediated communication tools frequently lack a good mechanism for representing authority; usually, all communications must flow through a designated autocratic "moderator" or editor. Although this method of facilitating group discussions is appropriate in some circumstances, it is ineffective in others. As students experimented with the nature of participation and the balance of control, they indicated a desire for a structure that could facilitate conversations. As new communities of practice develop, they will need common methods for governing conversations to enhance learning within and through CMC environments.

Crowding

A limited number of people could communicate effectively at any one time on ArtView. When the rooms or spaces around a particular artwork became crowded, people started private conversations, started another group, or limited the number of people they allowed into a conversation. Limiting the number of people involved in a conversation mitigated some of the confusion resulting from too many simultaneous strands of conversation.

Several users felt that limiting the number of people in a conversation was not enough and that limits should be imposed on the number of contributions that could be accepted by the network at a time. Reading conversations, understanding who initiated what, and maintaining conversations in the chat spaces were difficult. However, the participants who lobbied for a more structured and controlled approach realized that structure and control would come at a price. Slowing down the momentum of the conversation through some form of limits, for example, could decrease participation.

Spaces, the objects within them, and the events that transpire in them all encourage and afford certain behaviors (Gibson, 1977). The design of the space should suggest the type of activity or interaction associated with the space. People orient to these affordances and tend to adapt practices from the physical world to electronic space. To facilitate this transfer, virtual communities must be visible from the outside and provide cues for activities once people join a community (Dieberger, 1999). Though difficult to achieve, users of ArtView echoed this view. Many users were frustrated because they could not see who was in each room and what other group members were doing. Users also had difficulty following threads of conversations once they connected with a group.

Sources of Information

In addition to participating in real-time chat conversations, ArtView users also accessed another information source—the information box (see Figure 3.3). Museum Web sites usually provide only placards with the name, artist, and date of an artwork. ArtView's information boxes could contain background information, expert critiques, other visitors' comments, and guiding questions for viewing the paintings. Students could read as much or as little of the supporting documentation as they wished. Most people felt that notes left by other patrons added to their understanding of the artwork:

> *Martin:* The experience is most worthwhile if I'm with other people who open up new ideas and directions of scrutinizing the piece. I personally am not able to have this dialogue with myself. The right questions rarely occur to me.
>
> *Ben:* I like to know how old an object is, its purpose, something about the artist, general factual information, how it was constructed, and how it operated.

Having visitors leave a permanent annotation or record online in ArtView enriched information exchange and refined dialogues (see chapter 5). Nevertheless, students did not always focus their discussions or take advantage of the resources that were available to them. Many students referred to the information box only briefly during the online sessions. Participants wanted background information and links to other resources to be available, but reading that information during the chat sessions prevented them from participating in the conversations. Several students suggested that because the information resources and the live chat feature were in competition, users perhaps could be given time to read the text information on their own before engaging in a dialogue with other visitors about the artwork. In fact, social interactions in museum settings are usually more important than reading; museum patrons usually read about an artwork or an exhibit either before or after a visit to a museum (Carr, 1999).

Although the conversation channel was the preferred source of information for ArtView users, students also had suggestions for improving the information box accompanying each image. They recommended increasing the amount and type of information available by adding more thorough explanations of the artworks, the artists, and the period in which the works were created; more insights from art historians; links to similar or objects (online and in the museum); and links to other online resources. One student suggested that the ArtView designers needed to maximize the linking and communication capabilities of the computer. Although students did not have enough time during their session to read the information in the text box, they felt that this resource could be redesigned to help visitors understand art pieces in more depth at some other time.

Loss of Aesthetic Presence

Both the 2D and 3D versions of ArtView were responses to the traditional museum experience and built on the experience of visiting a museum. Before using ArtView, visitors identified what they felt were the typical or quintessential aspects of the museum experience—in other words, what they liked about visiting physical museums. Many of their comments reinforced findings from earlier studies. Recurring comments were that the museum experience is very personal in nature and that it provides visitors with a feeling of freedom. One visitor cited "escaping into therapeutic solitude" as a favorite aspect of the museum experience. Other participants noted the potential for quiet contemplation and yet also recognized the museum as a space teeming with life. For these visitors, the museum experience combines both personal and social elements, but the balance between these forces should be self-determined. For instance, visitors remarked that they liked to join guided tours but also have the option to leave the tours before they ended. Museum visitors also wanted to choose whether they participated (actively or passively) in conversations with others.

Participants in our studies liked the physical space of the museum—the large, high-ceilinged rooms, the interconnecting hallways, and the layouts that encouraged the feeling of personal exploration in a public setting. Visitors in our studies appreciated "roaming around exploring the museum." They welcomed the freedom of choice to make decisions weighed by personal tastes. For one visitor, the physical museum space should allow for an overview of opportunities for engagement with artworks:

> *Pam:* I like being able to pan around the room, spot a piece from afar, and gradually discover it as I walk toward it.

When asked to describe what they liked best about physical visits to the museum, visitors cited the opportunity to physically "interact" with an "authentic" work of art and to experience attributes such as scale, brushwork, lighting, and color. They also noted the importance of viewing artworks from different distances and angles. Finally, museum visitors said they enjoyed the ambiance of the museum space itself, along with the careful planning that goes into the display of artworks within the museum gallery (such as lighting and arrangement):

> *Michael: [What I like best about my experience in art museums is]* the presence of paintings—the color, size, texture that is lost in reproductions. *[I enjoy]* the act of walking around through spaces which are, hopefully, well-designed and complement the art that is displayed.

Conclusion

One of the greatest potentials of computer-mediated communication tools is their ability to enhance learning conversations. In a museum context, learning conversations occur between visitors and objects (and the people or environments that these objects represent), between visitors, and between visitors and museum curators or guides. We discovered that technology can be used to increase the range and nature of these conversations about art.

Supplanting the museum experience is not an appropriate use of technology, but a carefully designed online environment can provide conversational tools that support the learning experience. Because ArtView cannot fully replicate the aesthetic details of artworks and cannot reproduce all the nuances of face-to-face discussions, students felt that the application should be used to supplement rather than replace the experience of viewing artwork in person. All participants felt that ArtView opened up new conversational and informational channels for understanding art pieces but that these channels could not replace the physical experience of engaging with the art itself.

The people who participated in our study were sensitive to the differences between viewing artworks in person versus viewing digitized images on a computer screen and felt that online venues could not convey the full aesthetic quality and details of artworks and the museum space itself.

ArtView provided tools that support learning conversations among students and a database that allows curators, group leaders, or instructors to customize the background or contextual information that supplements or supports the online conversations. The images in the chat rooms provided a focal point for discussions. Although ArtView lacked the opportunities for personal choice and interaction with real objects that museums provide and also tended to homogenize the artworks with its display limitations, most students felt that the quality and convenience of the online resources could help them to understand a particular piece and to learn how to discuss and interpret objects and artifacts.

But the mere presence of new ways of communicating does not guarantee that the resulting discourse constitutes a learning conversation. The students' experiences highlighted important differences between increasing participation and enhancing participation. In fact, power dynamics influence the interactions that take place in computer-mediated environments. As Susan C. Herring (1996) notes, computer-mediated communication interactions are not completely democratic. Subtle characteristics of language and implicit or explicit information about the identity of the participants can affect the ideas that are developed and the comments that are acknowledged or ignored. In such situations, centrality is tacitly biased toward those with assertive communication styles and perceived importance or expertise.

Much of the enthusiasm for anywhere, anytime computing ignores the advantages of face-to-face interaction. Because many of the social cues we use in face-to-face interactions are missing in online communications, individuals and groups that are using these technologies (and researchers who are studying them) need to reflect on their implications for all the relationships they mediate and to create norms or rules to foster the types of relationships that the stakeholders desire.

We can summarize our findings from our studies of using computer-mediated communication and collaborative virtual environment tools for learning conversations as follows:

- CMC may disrupt the natural flow of conversation and lead to misinterpretation by removing discourse from its context;
- Participants are sometimes overwhelmed by technology, task, and communication issues;
- Different modes of interaction afford different experiences within the information space;
- Artifacts and objects play an instrumental role in mediating group activities;
- New social protocols need to be established for people to work effectively in CMC environments;
- CMC masks social cues and cultural differences;
- CMC does not guarantee increased participation and interaction among colleagues;
- Lack of social cues in CMC enables some people to become antagonistic toward others compared to copresent communication;
- Some people need more structure and guidance than others;
- Differences in participation rates are due to personal choice, time constraints, inadequate access, and fear of being judged;
- CMC can accommodate flexible communication patterns.

Allowing groups to collaborate and have successful social interactions over computer networks is a goal of software designers, but using technology to facilitate learning conversations does not automatically produce communication and understanding. Designers need to consider a number of variables that affect the quality of the users' experiences, including issues of trust, coordination, participants' networks, social cues, and other social conventions. Designers need to provide structures to support these new forms of interactions online rather than simply trying to replicate face-to-face interactions.

Collaborative virtual environments in themselves cannot ensure that the discussion group will remain focused on the central issue being addressed. The presence of other participants online, the way that objects are organized, and other design factors shape the ways that people respond to others in virtual spaces (Munro, Hook, & Benyon, 1999). Although communication media can shape and channel the kinds of group interactions that develop, learners need to be involved in ongoing conversations with competent partners who share similar interests and commitments. The challenge for designers of these technologies is to create simple environments that foster complex, supportive interactions.

4

Blurring Boundaries: A Study of Ubiquitous Computing

Bernard R. Gifford and Noel D. Enyedy (1999, p. 189) have drawn on activity theory to develop activity-centered design (ACD), a new model for computer-supported collaborative learning that is constructed on the premise that learning is "a complex process in which an individual's cognition is defined by its relation to the material setting and the forms of social participation encouraged by these settings." ACD builds on current attempts to integrate activity theory with other approaches, including situated learning (Lave & Wenger, 1991), learning community (Wenger, 1998), and collaborative learning (Bannon, 1989; Crook, 1989; Dillenbourg, 1999; Koschmann, 1996; Light & Light, 1999). Within an ACD framework, as in all social constructivist approaches, learning is conceived of as a social process that depends on shared task orientation and successful negotiation of meaning to achieve shared objectives and interaction among a group of learners.

As is discussed in chapter 1, an ecological perspective on learning views an organism's activity as always embedded within an environment (Nardi, 1996a, 1996b; Nardi & O'Day, 1999). Therefore, an ecological approach to studying collaborative learning technologies (Bronfenbrenner, 1989; Crook, 1989; Gibson, 1979) recommends that spaces be designed to support collaborative opportunities. Understanding computer-supported collaboration, however, poses considerable challenges for researchers and designers.

Wireless computer-mediated learning environments may support a constructive learning process by helping students find and organize information, construct their understandings in an appropriate context, and then communicate those understandings to others in other contexts. As is described in the next sections, the introduction of wireless laptop computers has transformed learning-related activities and thereby affected the physical settings of computing as well as the forms of social participation that occur within those settings. Wireless computers also support just-in-time learning, an adaptation of just-in-time inventory, a successful industry technique that delivers parts and finished products at precisely the time at which they are needed, which greatly decreases warehousing costs (Schoor, 1995). In education, students may receive context-appropriate information or complete a skill-building task at the most appropriate teachable moment.

Nomad: Research on Wireless Computing

To trace how wireless, pervasive computing affects the learning experience, Cornell's Human-Computer Interaction Group—through Nomad, a project funded by the Intel Corporation and Microsoft—introduced laptop computers with wireless network access to an undergraduate communication class of forty-five students. With the students' consent, all their Web browsing and communication activities throughout the semester were recorded through a proxy server.

In the classroom, students were encouraged and often required to use their wireless laptop computers to complete in-class assignments and to follow lectures oriented toward or anchored in particular Web sites (Abowd, Pimentel, Kerimbaev, Ishiguro, & Guzdial, 1999). The course incorporated several types of classroom interaction, including group activities, lectures, presentations, group discussions, and collaborative and experiential learning activities. Assignments included regular contributions to a class bulletin board, individual reflection papers, a midterm exam, and group projects.

As payment for participating in the study, students received laptop computers that were enabled for wireless local area networks (LANs). Data were collected on the students' use of the laptop computers and the wireless network from multiple sources, including Internet and e-mail usage, pre- and postcourse surveys, personal time-use diaries, individual and group interviews, and observational notes taken by researchers.

In reviewing survey data, tracking data, and students' journals and papers about their experiences with ubiquitous computing devices, we identified four recurrent themes related to students' perceptions and use of the technologies (Gay & Bennington, 2003). Students felt that mobile computing devices

- Gave them freedom from the constraints of space and time,
- Provided a level of pervasive access that resulted in temptation and addiction,
- Diverted their attention from classroom activities and relations, and
- Helped mediate community participation and classroom interactions.

Freedom from the Constraints of Space and Time

The mobile computer allowed students to study and communicate in many physical locations. Throughout students' journals and open-ended survey questions run themes of boundary crossing, blurring, and collapse. Activities that were previously closely bound to a particular location and time could be engaged in from a variety of spaces, social settings, and times.

Not only were the laptops mobile, which allowed students to carry them to various places around and off campus, but the wireless network afforded access to the Internet and other communication tools from numerous places across campus, including cafeterias, corridors, and outdoor areas. As one student noted in his journal, "The wireless aspect of this machine gives me more options of places to be during the day." Students no longer had to rely on the limitations of desktop-bound computers to do course-related work.

Building on the HCI Group's previous work with mobile computing (e.g., Gay, Rieger, & Bennington, 2002; Gay, Stefanone, Grace-Martin, & Hembrooke, 2002), we were particularly interested in identifying the ways in which mobility and ubiquity facilitated the blurring of space- and time-dependent boundaries among classroom, library, home, and recreational spaces. We found that as these temporal and spatial boundaries blurred, so did the social roles, communal expectations, norms, behaviors, and types of interactions that were associated with those spaces (Cho, Stefanone, & Gay, 2002).

Students talked about computer applications, particularly e-mail and instant messaging, in terms of the "freedom" they afforded from spatial and temporal constraints. Freedom from constraints of location and time shaped students' experiences of computing and also of the settings and times in which they used computers. Within the physical and social setting of the classroom, access to computer resources that were not directly related to the course disrupted face-to-face interactions and raised a number of issues directly relevant to computer-mediated communication in educational settings.

The metaphor of "freedom from" the restraints of space and time pervaded students' discussions, interviews, and journal entries on how access to these machines transformed their computing habits:

> For approximately four months [the length of the course], I have been developing patterns of use for my mobile computer that are unlike my previous computing experiences. Mobile computing unchained me from my stationary computer at home and allowed me to spend more time on campus. . . . My activities were transformed by the mobile computer. I had instant access to a steady stream of information—no more running to computer labs for a quick check of my e-mail when on campus. I can stay put in the library or my office and not waste time waiting on line for a free computer. . . . All this freedom and saved time translated into a significant increase in the amount of time I spent computing and accomplishing tasks in pursuit of my education.

> These tools [the laptops and wireless access] have offered me increased freedom over the course of the semester. The freedom is not the equivalent of increased free time, but rather the freedom is the increased opportunity to make choices as to how I choose to participate in class, complete assignments, and conduct my usual computer-related activities.

> With the laptop, I was able to check e-mail, read class articles, post to the class bulletin board, or do anything else on the Internet in one of the libraries or academic buildings without having to plug into a wall. This gave me much more freedom and flexibility to connect myself to the Internet when I wanted to regardless of my location.

Students associated the freedom offered by mobile computers with freedom of choice—the opportunity to choose tools, activities, and the time and method for engaging with others. The mobility of the laptops and the network made it possible for them to select the most convenient environments for engaging in coursework that required the computer and an Internet connection. No longer were their options limited to specific locations where networked computers and other resources were available.

Students offered interpretations of the kind of freedom the wireless laptop offered. Having wireless access enabled them to take part in online activities that they felt that they could not participate in without constant access:

Over the course of the semester, I transformed from a Wall Street onlooker to a serious trader in the stock market. As a user in the wireless community, I had the capabilities to track the movements of the market all day. It is crucial for any trader in today's market atmosphere to have access to real-time information at any given time. I had wanted to open an online account for months, but I was always wary of my inability to check the success of my portfolio during the day. There is a direct correlation between my being a user in the wireless community and my ability to buy and sell securities on the stock market. Being a user allowed me to do something in my life that I had wanted to do for quite a while. Thus, being a user improved my quality of life, a goal of wireless technology.

I use the computer a lot. It is interesting in that the usage for the most part is focused on two applications—the browser and the e-mail client. This is a far cry from the way I used to use the computer back when I owned a 486 to start off. Then it was the use of the machine to run things like, well, games. As the years progress and after discovering the Internet, my usage has gradually shifted toward the Internet connection rather than the use of the computer as its own stand-alone machine.

Students interpreted freedom mainly in terms of individual choice— choice of location in which to work, choice of task, choice of tool, and choice of person with whom to communicate. Rarely, however, did they view the technology as providing freedom from the computer or from the virtual world. In fact, a number of students understood the freedom that they gained from wireless laptops as the ability to use the computer more often, to surf the Web more thoroughly, and to use a wider array of communication tools. In other words, computing freedom in students' eyes meant introducing computing into more aspects (physical, social, and academic) of their everyday lives, rather than using the computer in a way that gave them more time away from computing. The laptops and wireless network were tools that allowed them to transcend the constraints of the physical world. For most students, such transcendence was desirable, and the choice to use the laptop was obvious.

Pervasive Access, Temptation, and Addiction

From the log data, we discovered that students spent three to seven hours per day on the Internet. Much of this time was spent contacting friends, family, and others either through e-mail or instant messaging. This desire to connect with others and maintain relationships with others informs other themes that were common in students' talk about the technology—

namely, temptation and addiction. Students discussed the temptation of communication tools and the Internet and their difficulty in resisting them either in class or when doing school-related work. Many actually referred to addiction to the laptops, instant messaging, and e-mail. Some students viewed the ability to engage in multiple activities as useful, but other students were not optimistic. One student wrote:

> When I go to the library, my goal is to study, and I often found access to the Internet through the wireless network to be distracting.

Still another student described how her involvement with e-mail has grown significantly since she received her wireless laptop:

> In my prelaptop years, I would be satisfied with having checked my mail three times a day—morning, afternoon, evening. Now that I can check my mail all over campus, without waiting in lines, . . . I do it around twenty-five times a day—five times in the morning, ten times in the afternoon, and ten times in the evening. I'm telling you, mobile wireless computers have increased my e-mail usage by 1000 percent. Sad fact: I've even found myself signing up for more newsletters just so I can receive more e-mails. Crazy, huh? Techies.com has a wonderful newsletter even though I don't understand a word of their techie language. Even sadder fact: I've checked my e-mail five times while writing this paragraph!
>
> [The wireless laptop] allowed me to obtain many multimedia programs that came in the form of games, stock tickers, news reports, and communication tools (chat boards, instant messenger, etc.). These programs intrigued me but would affect my studying at times in the library or other work-conducive environments. When studying for a test or doing other reading, I would find myself splitting my normal study time between these entertaining multimedia tools and academic study. As a result, I saw a decrease in my productivity that reminded me of the drawing power of TV and the will power needed to abstain from its broadcasts when it came time to study. As result, I forced myself to erase these multimedia programs from my hard drive, making sure that the only remaining programs available to me were those used for academic purposes. Still, I could not erase my access to the Internet or increase my will power. I found myself purposefully leaving this tool at home when going to study.

Students claimed that mobile computers freed them from the constraints of physical location, but the ubiquitous access that is provided by these devices produced a new demand on the users—the need to control the impulse to communicate or Web browse. Some students found that they needed to force themselves to eliminate the sources of temptation from their laptops or even avoid using their laptops altogether to get their work done:

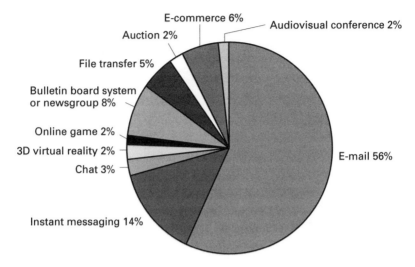

Figure 4.1
Students' use of laptop networking capabilities

> I take the mobile computer to the library to do work. In situations like this, I wonder whether the presence of a mobile computing device actually helps me in my studies. The wireless Internet capabilities are more distracting than useful. I constantly check e-mail or the Web. It takes a lot of restraint to concentrate on the work at hand.

One student went so far as to stop using his laptop and home desktop for a week to see how dependent he was on computer-mediated communication tools such as e-mail and instant messenger and whether his use of these tools kept him from doing his academic work:

> I was quite surprised when, during this week, I was able to get all my homework done on time as well as get more sleep each night. Writing papers and typing things were an inconvenience, but I trekked to the computer labs to perform these functions and still ended up with more time than I had before.

Students took great advantage of the networking capabilities of the wireless laptops. Analysis of the usage logs and the students' own reports showed that the most frequently used applications were e-mail and Internet browsers (figure 4.1). Instant messenger and other synchronous communication tools were also popular tools and became more popular over the course of the semester. The percentage of students self-reporting frequent

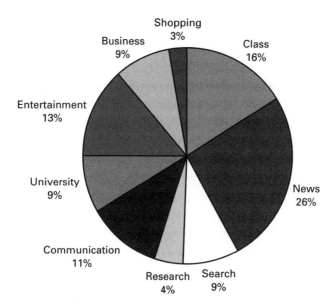

Figure 4.2
Students' URL browsing, by category

use of synchronous communication tools was 38.7 percent at the beginning of the semester and 53.6 percent by the end.

Of the 1.7 million unique uniform resource locators (URLs) recorded during the course of the semester, we categorized the content represented by nearly 2,000 URL hosts, which accounted for approximately 87 percent of the total URLs that were browsed by students (figure 4.2). Students used their laptops in their undergraduate communication course but were free to use the laptops as they wished—including for work in other courses, entertainment employment-related tasks, and social activities.

We found differences in the content of URLs that were browsed by men and women. Women were nearly three times as likely to use search engines as men. They also accessed sites that were associated with messaging and communication (such as Web-based e-mail and instant messaging) three times as often as men. Men typically frequented finance, sports, and entertainment sites more often than the women in the study.

Along with Web browsing and e-mail, some students observed that live chats had become an integral part of their lives:

One specific change that I noticed throughout the course of the semester was my discovery of AOL Instant Messenger. . . . Before this semester, I have never spent any time chatting live with my friends and relatives. However, throughout the past several months, IM has become part of my daily routine.

My communication with my friends and family definitely increased over the semester. . . . Now I am able to stay in touch with the events going on in Canada, while remaining a student in America. My laptop has given me a stronger connection to the people that are most important in my life.

Diverting Attention from Classroom Activities and Relations

One key purpose of the wireless study was to explore ways to use wireless laptops to augment classroom instruction. Along with an increased number of locations in which they could engage in computing activities, students described a transformation of their classroom experiences. The possibilities of what they could do during class meetings were expanded, and some uses were better, educationally, than others:

Students can take notes during class and already have them digitally in their computers. The student can also follow and participate online with the professor. Further research can be done during class discussions, the class can log on, and the research that a student searches diligently for can go along with the student wherever.

I could sit in a lecture and take notes as the professor spoke or even access notes from a course Web site that coincided with that day's lecture. For a person like myself—who often retains little from lectures when I am constantly note taking—this tool aided in my ability to retain important in-class information.

In class, students are on the laptops engulfed in what they are looking at, whether it is e-mail, the Internet, or course related. I found it frustrating at times because people are reading e-mail or another Web page instead of interacting in group discussions.

Freedom and choice became influential scripts that shaped students' tool use in the course, particularly through their ability to participate individually in and identify with multiple communities. Choice was evident even in the classroom, when students often communicated with others using instant messaging and e-mail and surfed the Web. The students were using the computers to communicate, but they did not necessarily communicate with other class members. Students often communicated with nonclass members during class sessions. Engaging in separate, individual-ized computer-mediated communication and information-seeking activi-ties with various communities outside the class tended to conflict with collaborative interactions within the classroom.

We were particularly interested in examining whether the computers helped support community-based learning approaches or disrupted the learning environment. In our studies of the tracking data, we analyzed log files to look at patterns of activity and actual behavior in these complex classroom and lab environments (Gay, Stefanone, Grace-Martin, & Hem-brooke, 2002). A number of students mentioned in their journals and dur-ing interviews that they felt that they could multitask. They felt that they had better concentration when they were doing more than one thing:

> I found that I could listen to the lecture, check my e-mail, or browse the Internet.

> I used the Internet in class to look along with the guest speaker about Active Worlds [a virtual reality online environment]. The tool, the Internet, allowed me to visually understand what the speaker was talking about, and I could use the software hands on.

> The laptop in general makes me feel like I can do several different tasks in one sitting. There has never been a session in which I didn't have multiple windows minimized on my desktop menu bar and I didn't constantly switch from one task to the next. For instance, during the thirty minutes or so that I've been working on this paper, I remembered that I needed to send out an electronic birthday card to a friend. With the click of a mouse, I did it, before I could for-get it was her birthday today. On the other hand, my multiple minimized win-dows get me into trouble. A couple minutes ago, the familiar new mail icon for Eudora popped up at the same time that I was hit with a train of thought for this paragraph. I've had to fight the urge to click over to Eudora, knowing that I could get lost in an e-mail and lose a paragraph on my paper.

In two of our studies (Gay, Stefanone, Grace-Martin, & Hembrooke, 2002; Grace-Martin & Gay, 2001), we found that the longer the browsing sessions, the lower the final grade tended to be. In some instances, longer browsing sessions may be more distracting than shorter ones. Finally, we found robust divided-attention effects when students were allowed to multitask during a typical lecture. Again, their browsing style was found to correlate with performance on the follow-up exam.

These reports were replicated in a follow-up study of divided attention in the classroom (Gay & Hembrooke, 2002). Although students think that

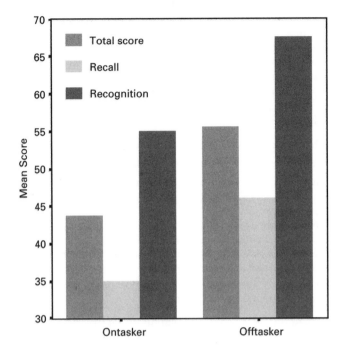

Figure 4.3
Recall and recognition scores during open and closed laptop sessions

they can attend to several things at once, we found that they had difficulties monitoring their Web browsing and online behavior. Students who became engaged in a particular task online did worse on recall and recognition tests than students who did superficial browsing (figure 4.3). In other words, short browsing did not produce debilitating effects on performance, but sustained browsing resulted in decreased performance.

Many students in the mobile computing study were ambivalent about the usefulness of Internet access and readily available communication tools in classroom settings. Several discussed their mixed feelings about the wireless laptops in their journals:

> Mobile computing positively contributing to class subject matter. . . . In other situations, the mobile computing distracted the class and me from the subject matter and class participation. When we use the mobile computing in class to do personal work and do not participate, this takes away from the purpose of the tool.

While CMCs are great tools, the fact that they're readily available makes them somewhat of a distraction as well. I see that fairly often in class students are chatting away with their friends through AOL Instant Messenger rather than paying attention to the lecture. . . . I admit to occasionally launching Instant Messenger during class as well. The temptation is difficult to resist. I am quite torn between my thoughts on CMC. The question is not whether or not they are useful and beneficial, since they unquestionably are, but rather, "When is their use justified and in what setting?"

Some students, however, found the pursuit of tangential activities in class useful or at the very least not distracting. The fact that students were able to use CMC software somewhat discretely during the lecture might have made these activities seem less disruptive to them:

With my laptop computer, I could and often did plan the rest of my day during lecture without distracting anyone around me—not even myself entirely—from the professor's words. Of course, I wouldn't dream of calling a friend with a cellphone from a lecture to say, "Hey, you want to have a beer after class?" But it's easy and expedient to send those same words in the same situation as an instant message or e-mail.

Although this student did not seem to feel that his use of the wireless laptop's communication tools were distracting or inappropriate, a number of students expressed concern that their constant access to the wireless network was turning their interactions with communication tools into an obsession. One student claimed that his "reliance on Instant Messenger is all encompassing." Another stated, "The pull of Internet browsing I find especially strong. . . . My Internet browsing has gotten so bad now that I can estimate the time when daily Web sites update their information. Browsing the Internet is truly an addiction."

Instead of building learning communities, the wireless laptops may have diverted the class from its original learning goals. Since students were simultaneously engaged in multiple communities during class time, they may have been subverting constructivist learning principles and goals. According to constructivist learning principles, shared attention to negotiating and pursuing objectives is central to effective learning. Behind the screens of their laptops, students could actively engage in note taking, instant messaging, e-mailing, and information seeking during the class period without the instructor or most other students perceiving what they were doing. The absence of formal rules regarding wireless laptop use likewise tacitly encouraged individuals to do as they "chose"—that is, pursue individual objectives. A student commented that "most of the class was engaging in multitasking during lecture," and observational notes support this claim. Students were thereby participating in and identifying with multiple divergent external communities and activities that were not class related (such as day trading, communicating with family and friends, and searching for personally relevant information). The shared practice that evolved in the class was individualized use of the laptops with often fragmented attention directed toward speakers, whether lecturers or other students, during class discussions. Even when carrying out group assignments in class, many groups worked individually, coming together at the last moment to compile individual contributions into a collective product.

In Christopher M. Hoadley and Noel Enyedy's (1999, p. 242) terms, when students engage in non-class-related tasks during class, tools create monologues within the social setting of the classroom. Students who engage in individually oriented tasks are diverted from the face-to-face dialogue that is afforded by the physical copresence of other students.

Another student admitted that she was often lured away from what was going on in class to use the network applications that were available to her on her wireless laptop:

> Multitasking during class divided my attention three ways among lecture, computing, and the classmates around me. I believe my computing reflected my short attention span, as I would switch back and forth from one application to another, while focusing on the happenings of lecture.

Another student used terminology that is revealing. Although she chose to use the wireless laptop's communication tools, she described herself as falling "victim" to their allure, as if she were not in control of her computer usage. She used passive language to explain that the computer, and not the way she herself used it, was bringing her "away from her studies," echoing the concerns about addiction noted previously by other students:

> With all the possible benefits this tool has to offer, I felt in some ways that it acted as a gateway to many activities that brought me away from my studies. In some classes, for instance, when the lecture information was not available through my laptop, I found myself using e-mail constantly. . . . In similar instances, I fell victim to searching the Web for unrelated nonacademic information that took my focus off the class.

The passive stance toward the wireless computer expressed by this student suggests that some students feel that they are absolved from taking responsibility for their own actions. The student quoted below also suggested that her studies were adversely affected by her computer use because students were not given rules on how to use their wireless laptops:

> Maybe some restrictions or guidelines when we were issued the computer would have prevented me from using this tool in an unproductive manner.

Another student also felt that the class might have benefited from restrictions on laptop usage, although she preferred the idea of having students themselves set their own limitations:

> I like the suggestion made in class the other day: the class as a whole should make a list of rules, and everyone should abide by them.

In some ways, the establishment of collaboratively constructed social norms and rules of interaction may actually foster rather than inhibit a collaborative learning environment and a sense of freedom in students. Rather than finding themselves adrift in a sea of communication options, students who follow mutually agreed on rules can resist temptation by formulating a framework for use and by linking tool use to specific, learning-related objectives.

Mediating Community Participation and Classroom Interactions

Because students made frequent use of e-mail, instant messaging, and the bulletin board, we decided to examine in more detail the actual role played by these tools in structured learning settings. These tools can help foster relationships and activities in the classroom and build a community, but the same tools can divert attention from the classroom (Cho, Stefanone, & Gay, 2002).

Consider, for example, the social navigation achieved through students' use of the class listserv and message board. From the beginning of the semester, students and faculty used the class listserv and the class discussion board to recommend Web sites to each other. The research team looked at discussion board threads and the listserv for explicit recommendations of URLs posted by students and for subsequent "hits" to those Web sites by others in the class.

Table 4.1
Frequency of students' URL recommendations and consequent hits over time

Time (22-day blocks)	URLs Recommended	Consequent hits
1	27	3849
2	11	963
3	5	85
4	6	0
5	0	0

An analysis of the discussion board and the class listserv revealed that students functioned well in general communication when they conveyed content of interest to the entire class. The bulletin board was used primarily for discussions that were focused on particular class topics, whereas the class listserv was used more for general announcements, such as posting interesting URLs. We found a significant difference between the number of hits on a Web site before and after a classmate's recommendation (Cho et al., 2002). In other words, when students recommended a URL on either the discussion board or the listserv, other students in the social network of the class followed and explored the referenced URL (table 4.1). The phenomenon of social navigation was evident, indicating strong community participation. Examining discussion-board threads and the class listserv identified explicit recommendations of URLs that were posted by students. For each URL recommended, the total number of page views (measured by the number of Web pages) by other class members and the number of unique visitors to the URL were quantified using the proxy-server log file.

The results indicate that network participants in this computer-supported collaborative learning community were followed the social recommendations that were made by some actors more than those made by other actors. We hypothesized that status differences were operating, with some students having more prestige than others. However, as the semester progressed, many students did not post messages to the board. We also noticed that less prestigious or less central actors were more likely to post toward the end of the semester. While timeliness, usability, relevance, and sufficiency of information may be crucial factors determining the degree to which students learn something out of these social navigation practices

(Webb, 1989), social influences, in the form of network prestige effects, may have strongly affected the extent to which information posted in these tools was actually shared by peers in this learning community.

As the semester progressed, groups began to e-mail more to group members and communicate more within their project teams than they communicated with the whole class. Although the group projects were assigned at the beginning of the semester, log files indicated that groups did not begin serious work on them until after the middle of the semester. After the midterm examinations, communications among students became increasingly task oriented. Tools that were designed for large audiences were replaced with more personal, individual communication tools—namely, e-mail and group discussion boards. The pattern of interaction and use of tools changed as the type of work or activity changed.

That communication outside students' groups dropped off was not surprising considering the type of assignment and the time of the semester. In the second analysis, we analyzed only e-mails that students who were selected as group leaders sent to other members of their group and to members outside their respective groups. E-mails to members within their groups increased sharply, nearly doubling between the middle of the semester and the end, while e-mail with members of the class outside their groups decreased to nearly none.

That communication within project groups increased over the semester is not surprising. What is surprising, however, is the degree to which most of the communication seemed to filter through group leaders, whose role was best served by the social communicative benefits of e-mail (such as being able to send an entire group the same message). The patterns that emerged indicate that tool use was differentially affected by the role that one assumed or was assigned with the group.

The social and communication network structures that were revealed by our analysis of e-mail and discussion board submissions resemble each other. Figure 4.4 represents communication structures in the e-mail network sociogram and the discussion board sociogram. These two networks were derived from a social network analysis of interactions throughout the semester. In these sociograms of the communication class, nodes represent social actors, and lines between them show the communication linkages. The lines are weighted, meaning that thick lines represent strong ties (more

E-mail network sociogram   **Discussion board sociogram**

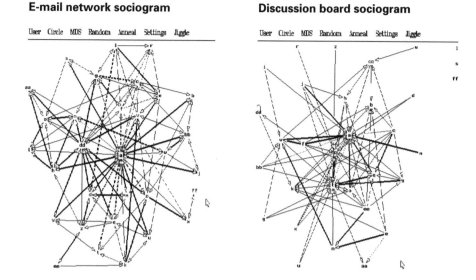

Figure 4.4
Communication structures of the e-mail network sociogram and the discussion board sociogram

frequent interactions between dyads). As shown in figure 4.4, some students held strongly central positions, while others were located in peripheral positions at the edge of the map.

Three social isolates appear in the discussion board network, whereas in the e-mail network every actor is connected to at least one social tie. On average, members in both networks contain a similar number of network partners (e-mail average = 5, discussion board average = 4.8) and interaction frequencies (e-mail = 12.97 messages sent, discussion board = 7.3 messages sent). Students used e-mail more frequently than they used the discussion board. A calculation of network densities (measured by the total number of existing linkages divided by the total number of possible ties) indicated that students in the e-mail network were more connected (.167) than those in the discussion board network (.085).

Some students were ignored by other class members, and other students were late in participating, issues that need to be addressed in the design and evaluation of a successful virtual online community of learning. From a practical point of view, these findings stress that a teaching staff should employ early interventions (such as identifying peripheral members in a learning community as soon as possible) to help students become active and productive class members.

Because the class was an upper-level course in a particular discipline, many students had already taken courses together. As members of another closely related community, that of Cornell University students, they had established social ties with other students, a social network overlaid on the arbitrarily constructed network of the class. We discovered that rather than making new social ties or reaching out to unfamiliar class members, many students continued to communicate with their own preexisting social groups.

Computing behavior is dynamic and will evolve to accommodate the changing needs and demands of the people who are working in particular conditions or situations. First, students' computing behavior is, and will be, influenced by classroom structure and resources. For example, throughout the semester, communication and interaction among class and group members were encouraged. Students used their laptops primarily as social communication tools, both in relaying information and in participating in asynchronous communication. As the structures within the class transitioned from the class community to the group communities, students' subsequent communications reflected that change, as evidenced by the decrease in e-mails to members outside students' immediate work groups.

Conclusion

Introducing a wireless computer network to students to use during school hours highlighted the ambiguity of roles, objectives, and norms regarding tool use in the classroom, particularly during lectures and presentations. We found that the wireless laptops—particularly their communication applications—disrupted classroom interactions by diverting individuals' attention from classroom activities and by sometimes interfering with face-to-face dialogue. Students were aware that when they used these tools, they violated implicit cultural norms regarding work habits, social roles, and behavioral expectations, such as listening to speakers and responding to peers in class discussions (Gay & Bennington, 2003). Instead of building learning communities, this technology may have interfered with the creation of temporary and long-term shared objectives, goals, and interactive norms, which are critical to effective collaborative learning (Crook, 1994; Wenger, 1998) and to the integrity of collective activity (Kuutti, 1996).

This diversity of tools, subjects, objectives, and activities raises the issue of whether and how to design and facilitate the communal or social-contextual features of tool implementation and use in learning environments (Gay & Bennington, 2003). For collaborative learning, in particular, shared frameworks, resources, and objectives are important for effective learning and need to be understood in terms of the learner's becoming a full participant in a community of practice. The achievement and maintenance of mutual understanding and shared resources comprise the process of "grounding" in collaborative education and can be significantly transformed by mediating tools (Baker, Hansen, Joiner, & Traum, 1999).

Students and faculty have limited visions of how systems should be integrated into learning environments. Classroom structure, tools, and tasks contribute to- and influence the experience of learning. In discussing collaborative learning environments, Hoadley and Enyedy (1999, p. 1) explain that different media constrain and enable certain types of interactions and certain processes for constructing and negotiating meaning through interaction and collaborative activity.

Although most educational environments are organized to favor independent knowledge acquisition and individual performance, classes need to be organized to take advantage of new technologies for knowledge building. As the results here indicate, students within a collaborative learning environment readily recognize and utilize social communication tools to exchange information. Introducing wireless computing resources into learning environments can potentially effect the development, maintenance, and transformation of learning communities. Ubiquitous mobile computing allows students to engage in learning-related activities in diverse physical locations, to work on projects supported by multimedia resources at the point of learning, to communicate with distant collaborators, and to access information networks anywhere, anytime. Wireless computing technologies can potentially enhance social learning and can augment the acquisition of tacit knowledge that is part and parcel of socialization into communities of practice.

However, learning activities are complex systems of interactions, and the benefits of ubiquity and mobility can easily be lost if that complexity is not appreciated and understood. In particular, we need to understand better

- New social protocols and norms for computer-mediated communication environments, particularly in the classroom;
- Ways that researchers and designers can provide structure and guidance for participants, especially at the beginning of a project or activity;
- Ways that tools can be adapted to meet the needs of people using them at a particular time for a specific task;
- Social variables such as gender, leadership, and peer respect.

In both an activity theory approach and a constructivist and community-based learning approach, shared objectives and collective task orientation are critical constituent features of productive interactions (Baker, Hansen, Joiner, & Traum, 1999; Tolmie & Boyle, 2000; Wenger, 1998). The freedom and individual choice that frequently informed students' tool use in this study potentially undermine such a shared orientation. This phenomenon of divergence draws attention to the need for researchers to look at tools in relation to one another—that is, to the relationship between face-to-face communication and mediated communication spaces and to the relationship among the different applications that are available through wireless communication tools.

5

Designing for Context-Aware Computing

As computing devices recede further and further into the background of everyday life (Norman, 1998), researchers and designers are asking new questions about the functionality, usability, and relevancy of computers and the context in which these devices will be used. Understanding users and the ways that they will to incorporate these new tools into their lives increasingly requires designers to learn lessons from cultural anthropology, sociology, information sciences, and psychology.

Similar to researchers who work in these other disciplines, those in the field of human-computer interaction must grapple with issues of validity— particularly the relevancy of an application, a system, a manipulation, or an intervention in a given setting with a given population. With the advent of "aware technologies," the notion of validity emerges in the form of a question: how can the construct of context be operationally defined?

Increasingly, this question is being addressed and debated by computer scientists, anthropologists, cognitive scientists, designers, sociologists, and information architects. The ubiquity of computing and the fluidity that comes with increasing mobility through mobile devices creates multiple levels of context. Just when the essence of context seems to have been captured, it separates yet again, like mercury on a mirrored surface.

In this chapter, we briefly review some of these new definitions of context in the realm of computing and extract some of their common arguments and structure. We then present a case study that illustrates a constructivist and iterative design approach to the development of a interactive context-aware tool at the Human-Computer Interaction Group at Cornell. This approach to the design and development of new context-based computer applications may be the best method for integrating context into these technologies—at least until we figure out a better way to contain the mercury or at least to differentiate the substance from the surface.

Context-Aware Computing

Context-aware computing is subsumed within the category of ubiquitous computing and includes familiar and relatively simple functions (such as traversing between various windows, cut-and-paste functions, and call forwarding), location-aware applications (which use infrared or global positioning technology to determine the location of the user to disseminate information that may or may not be of interest to the user), and even the futuristic world of intelligent sensors and appliances (such as aware lighting, talking refrigerators, and intelligent garbage cans). In every instance, the concept of context includes information that is intrinsic and extrinsic to the individual as well as the system. Understanding how these levels of context influence and impact computing is critical for the design of useful, effective aware technologies.

Three major theoretical approaches have been offered in this book thus far to explain contextual influences on behavior in general and on computing behavior specificly. In the first chapter, activity theory (Kuutti, 1996; Nardi, 1996a, 1996b) is reviewed. It posits that context emerges as a result of the activities that occur in a given setting. As the setting and the artifacts within the setting encourage different activities, these activities change, which thus changes the context in turn. Activity theorists recognize variables that are inherent to the individual (such as the goals and intentions of the user) and to the physical setting (such as other people and the artifacts that mediate the activities imposed on them).

Lucy Suchman's (1987) theory of situated action, originally developed as a theory of human cognition, suggests that cognition and planned activities are inexplicably connected and that both are by-products of the social and physical interactions that individuals have with and through their environments. Context is dynamic because the sequences of actions that are carried out in a given context are fluid and responsive to changes in social and physical settings.

Phenomenology, which is associated with the German philosopher Martin Heidegger (1992), holds that individuals make sense of the world through their participation in it. Action is a prerequisite to this understanding. Meaning is extracted directly from the information available in the environment; action and interaction are the tools by which this extraction process is made possible.

Central to all three of these theories is the connection between, on the one hand, participation and action and, on the other, understanding the context, whether the physical context or the capabilities of a particular tool. The theories focus on the individual and define context not as a defined set of properties but instead as an emergent, fluid attribute that is unleashed by the activities imposed on it. Thus, rather than a physical construct, context is "an operational term: something is 'in context' because of the way it is used for interpretation, not due to its inherent properties" (Winograd, 2001, p. 406).

Putting the Context in Context-Aware Computing

Until now, context has been characterized as relatively static and stable. The desktop workspace, whether at home or in the office, has kept context chained to a single location that is frequented usually by a single user. Context-aware applications challenge these traditional conceptions of space as a physical place and expand the repertoire of activities that might be performed with these new tools in the varied physical contexts in which they are used.

Developing relevant aware applications requires researchers to redefine *context* as a multidimensional construct that has overlapping and interacting layers. Thus, context includes the external physical context, the context that the individual brings to the situation, the context of the tool or device, the information context, and the context that is created by the activity itself. Defining these levels, the levels within each level, and the ways that they overlap with each other helps researchers identify how the individual interprets these concentric layers of context and therefore understands the tool's intended purpose.

Generic definitions of these contextual layers have been prescribed (Dey, Abowd, & Salber, 2001), but although such attempts underscore the importance of identifying contextual features, they typically have focused only on location and the identifying attributes of context. In addition, they fail to account for the dynamic nature of contextual influences. Given the complexity of context and the variable functionality that aware technologies could conceivably manifest, Saul Greenberg (2001, p. 260) argues that simple taxonomies may be "difficult or impossible for a designer/programmer to test a priori."

How, then, do we design effective context-aware technologies? First, we concur with Greenberg (2001) in that tools must be observed in the context for which they are intended. The case study discussed below illustrates this point well. Further, in designing any tool, an iterative, user-centered design approach is critical. In the rest of this chapter, we describe the entire developmental process that was involved in the design of a context-aware application for museums, MUSE. At each iteration of this developmental progression, multiple methods were used to assess functionality, users' understanding and conceptual maps, problems and disruptions, and satisfaction. With each successive iteration, different aspects of important contextual information emerged, and in the end, MUSE is in some ways very different from the initially designed application.

MUSE: Designing Context-Aware Computing Systems

In 1998, we began brainstorming ideas for developing MUSE, a context-aware technology application for museums. We had a couple of initial goals for this tool: we wanted to develop an application for use in an educational environment, and we wanted the tool to incorporate location awareness and to allow users to communicate with each other around objects and places. Another project on wireless mobile computing (the Nomad project discussed in chapter 4) had students use their laptops primarily for communicating and collaborating with other students. By extending the project's context to include social navigation, we felt that we could capitalize on this natural proclivity. In addition, we thought that a consensual interactive space might facilitate the interpretation of context and relevancy in a relatively novel application.

With these two constraints in mind, we introduced the notion of context-aware computing to a group of students who had been using mobile networked laptops for several months as part of the Nomad project. From this focus group, several themes and scenarios emerged, which fell into class-related and campus-related categories. Several ideas that were generated by the focus group centered around the notion of having professors and students share information both in and out of the classroom. Others included displaying campus events that were occurring at the user's location that day, communicating with others by leaving electronic notes at specific physical locations, and implementing an instant messaging system that could reveal user proximity in a visual manner.

Semaphore: A Context-Aware Collaborative Application

Semaphore is the Java application developed out of the Nomad mobile networked laptop trial. The Semaphore system had a centralized database and a small client application. For the first version of Semaphore, we defined context along three dimensions—location, date and time, and user. The database stored a collection of links to Web sites and documents. Each link was defined in terms of who created it, whether it was shared or private, what location it was associated with, and what its date and time range should be. The information that is associated with a context of use in this system is thus completely defined by the user. Having users interpret the relevance and meaning of a context is not typical of context-aware systems, which usually rely on system designers to do this work (Burrell, Treadwell, & Gay, 2000).

As soon as a user on the campus wireless network opened the client application, the application determined the user's physical location using a standardized simple network management protocol (SNMP). Then it contacted the database, filtered through the database's thousands of links, and returned and displayed only those that were relevant to the user's location and date and time context. In this sense, the application was an example of using context awareness as a method of filtering through information like a lens, bringing into focus what is relevant to the current environment (Pascoe, 1997).

Semaphore supported social navigation through a pull-down menu that users clicked on to access various Web sites and documents (figure 5.1). When the client application displayed links to the user, the shared-context links folder and the personal-context links folder were visible. The shared-context links folder contained links to Web sites or documents that had been configured by anyone with the proper permissions, such as a designated professor, department administrator, or student. These permissions

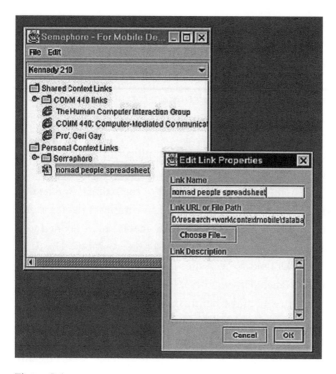

Figure 5.1
Semaphore's initial interface: a shared-context links folder and a
personal-context links folder

were determined on a location-by-location basis. For example, permission
to edit shared links could be granted to a professor to be used only in or
near her classroom. Shared-context links were viewed by everyone who en-
tered the location. These links could also be configured to appear only during a given time range. If the user chose to add a link that was stored on his
local computer, the link was automatically uploaded to a server so that it
was accessible to other users.

The personal-context links folder contained links to Web sites or documents that had been defined by the user and that could be viewed only by
him. This allowed the user to associate a different location with different
types of information that was relevant only to him. For example, a user
might add work-related links at his work location and links related to a
professional organization that he is involved with in the vicinity of the organization's office.

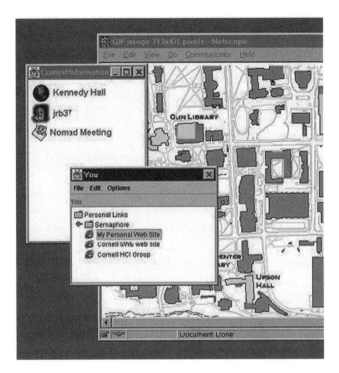

Figure 5.2
Semaphore's second interface: links organized by category

We released the Semaphore system to students to test on their laptop computers for one month. Interviews and focus groups conducted after the trial indicated that students felt that usability was good but that they wanted additional functionality—specifically, to be able to organize links to reflect meaningful structure. This finding is in keeping with William Mark's research findings (1999). In addition, students wanted to be able to form groups and share information. We felt that we could accommodate these focus-group requests by expanding the contextual features within the system.

The second version of Semaphore defined context in terms of categories like location, person, event, and group (figure 5.2). Each category had a set of links and files that were associated with it (objects) and that the user could access. A category object was displayed to the user when it became contextually relevant. For example, a location object appeared when a user was at the location, an event object appeared on the day of the event and at the location of the event, and a person object appeared when that person's wireless computer was nearby. To foster increased social navigation among participants, anyone could form a group, and any member of that group could add links to the group object. In this way, individuals could share information. Document annotation features were also added so that any user could associate notes with a document that other users could view when accessing the document through Semaphore.

Students were interviewed after they had used the revised version of Semaphore for three weeks. They had created both shared and personal links that reflected their own knowledge and associations with different locations on campus. Shared links that were associated with a location included Web sites for departments housed in a building and for classes that met in a building, bus schedules for buses that ran near a building, links to library information in the libraries, and links to local resources such as computer labs and dining halls. Personal links also reflected the users' context. Some users created work-related links that showed up only at their workplaces. For example, a student lab researcher added links to statistics pages that related to the local wireless network infrastructure. Among other things, the statistics page showed a list of other users who were at that location.

E-Graffiti

In the third generation of this prototype, we were interested in identifying the type of information that users associated with their context of use, the problems that they had in understanding location awareness, and the interesting and novel uses that they might devise for this type of system. The test system we designed, an application called E-graffiti, was like Semaphore in that it could detect the user's location on the Cornell campus wireless network. Relevant text notes were displayed based on the user's location and identity. Users were able to view only the notes associated with their current location. The application also allowed users to create notes and associate those notes with specific locations on the wireless network (figure 5.3). Users were able to post both public and private notes. Public notes were visible to anyone who logged onto E-graffiti at that location. Private notes were visible only to users who were chosen by the note writer (Burrell & Gay, 2001).

Figure 5.3
E-graffiti's interface

We asked fifty-seven students to evaluate the E-graffiti system for one semester. In this iteration, we tracked participants' usage patterns, logged all input into a database file, and asked participants to fill out a questionnaire at the termination of the project. The database contained the content of each note, the location that it was associated with, the date that it was created, and the user who created it. In addition, when users read or deleted notes, the action and the date and time were recorded in the database. The system also logged how frequently the E-graffiti system was used at various locations. Because the database logged information that was potentially private and sensitive, users were warned verbally in advance that the system would log their notes, they were required to sign informed-consent contracts, and they were shown a warning whenever they accessed the E-graffiti system.

The high number of participants and the long trial period that was allowed for evaluating the E-graffiti system resulted in rich data and valuable new insights. The logged data helped to support and clarify some of the underlying problems and confusion that were reported by users. A primary difficulty was users' relatively naïve understanding of location awareness. While users generally responded positively to the E-graffiti system, this positive response seemed to result more from the system's novelty than from its efficacy. Throughout the entire semester-long trial, users logged onto the system an average of only 7.6 times, usually from the same one or two locations on campus. Most notes were private, and their content seemed to have little relevance to the location from which they were generated. More digging indicated that most students were using E-graffiti for instant messaging.

These system limitations of E-graffiti seem to be an example of what Donald A. Norman (1983) refers to as the distinction between the conceptual model of a system (the designer's intent for the system) and the mental model of a system (the user's way of thinking about the system). In the case of E-graffiti, we tried to make the interface as intuitive and easy to use as possible by tapping into users' mental model of e-mail. Note templates included "To," "From," "Date," "Subject," and body fields, and each note had a small envelope icon that indicated whether it was new or old. In actual use, these features were more overpowering than we expected, and many students came to see E-graffiti as another form of e-mail. They saw the location-tracking feature as irrelevant or as a limitation because it prevented them from getting e-mail to its appropriate recipient. One user commented that she did not use E-graffiti much because "notes left for me at one location can't be picked up from another."

It's not surprising that users adopted an e-mail model and ignored E-graffiti's location-aware aspects. According to their previous experiences with communication technologies, an item of information goes from one individual (the sender) to another (the recipient). Location awareness was not a standard capability for the computers that these users had encountered. In the case of E-graffiti, we should have chosen a conceptual model that did not limit the user's concept of how to use the system. A better method might have been to use a campus map to organize the notes and attach them to locations on the map interface. The map would emphasize the location-aware aspect of the system and a conceptual model that suggests annotation rather than e-mail. By removing the private-note functionality, the temptation to resort to known communication models may have been lessened further.

Janet Fulk (1993) has demonstrated that social interactions influence be-havior and attitudes toward technology. We observed this in the way that students used E-graffiti as well as in the frequency that they used it—or rather, did not use it. Initially, members of the communication class were at a loss as to how they should use E-graffiti, but as soon as a few members of the class demonstrated a way to use E-graffiti, others quickly adopted it, and using E-graffiti as a chatting tool spread through social influence. We at-tempted to influence use socially in a similar way to encourage users to take advantage of the location-aware functionality. We did this by posting our own notes that did not follow the chatting model users had already demon-strated. For example, we posted notes that announced events happening at a particular location or that featured frequently asked questions about the facilities. A few users responded to our questions or posted similar notes.

Similarly, students did not seem motivated to use E-graffiti. In the ques-tionnaire, twenty-three users responded that their reason for not using E-graffiti was that too few other people were using it. One user summed it up by saying that E-graffiti "didn't seem like it was very useful since it wasn't very popular." The specific mediating factors in this effect might have been either the lack of critical mass borne from an imbalance in people who could make useful contributing notes (Grudin, 1988) or else the way that people conceptualized the system as a chat or communication tool.

From this round of evaluations, we concluded that students' limited un-derstanding about location-aware technologies resulted in vague notions about how to use such a system. Students reported in large numbers that they didn't think about information in terms of location, didn't know what notes to write, and didn't have anything to share with others at a location. Students used the E-graffiti system primarily as a synchronous chat tool, much like AOL's Instant Messenger. Because of the malleability of the sys-tem, users defaulted to a familiar mode of communication and interaction.

Although users could post notes of any kind, they did not have the time or energy to think extensively about location and the information that might be relevant to their current context. Users needed more directions and suggestions about unique ways to use the system. To resolve this issue, context-aware applications could be designed around a highly relevant contextual focus that certain user groups at that location would have a vested interest in—for example, paintings in an art museum or buildings on a campus tour.

CampusAware

To sharpen students' sense of campus locations, reduce some of their uncertainties, and heighten the relevance of context in synchronous electronic messaging, we created another iteration of the semaphore system that was a self-guided campus tour called CampusAware. In addition, we developed CampusAware for a hand-held personal digital assistant (PDA) that was equipped with a global positioning system for accurate location detection. Like its predecessor, all content in the system was created by the user. We hoped that students would find that the PDA allowed them to take greater advantage of locational context than the wireless laptop did.

Using the CampusAware system, a user could freely walk around campus (figure 5.4). The PDA was programmed to alert the user that information relevant to their location was available. In addition, users could virtually "tag" a location with information they chose to contribute. Later on, other users could encounter these tagged notes and potentially benefit from the shared information. Again, the idea of collectively gathering information from users and using it to influence and inform other users was incorporated to foster social interaction. Thirty-five students took the campus tour with this device. All notes and their locations were logged for future analysis. Users also filled out a survey when they returned from the tour.

Unlike users of E-graffiti, users of CampusAware were highly motivated to contribute and found the notes that other users wrote to be interesting. Each user walked around the campus with the system for thirty to sixty minutes. In that amount of time, users, on average, left 3.7 notes, with an average note length of about seventy-three characters. After the initial evaluation, users had collectively contributed 129 new notes: seventy notes were factual, and fifty-nine notes were opinions or advice. These opinion or advice notes represented a departure from the comments that are normally associated with a traditional campus tour, and users felt that leaving this kind of note was important. As one user noted: "I want other students to try out some of the fun things I did on campus but was never told about when I went on the tours."

Among the factual notes was a subcategory of notes that described activities that take place at a specific space. CampusAware users wrote thirty-three such notes. For example, one user wrote, "Day Hall is the center for

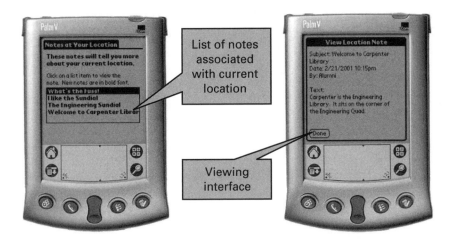

Figure 5.4
CampusAware's interface

most of the administration done on campus. Many times throughout the year socially conscious students may hold demonstrations outside this hall."

Results from the survey that users filled out after their tours indicated that notes contributed by an unofficial source, whether students or other insiders, were valued more than the official factual notes that the designers posted to have something in the database for users to read at the start of the trial. The insider notes were primarily informal, sometimes opinionated, and often humorous. One user commented, "Notes that kind of gave an 'insider's' perspective were quite interesting." Another user said, "I found the personal, insider notes from other students useful and informative." A third user stated, "I think when people come on a tour, the thing they are looking for is not only information about the school but real advice from the students who go there." This evidence provides some justification for opening systems to this type of user feedback: content that is created by insiders is unique and is well received.

Given that students generally were unmotivated to contribute to the E-graffiti system, we wondered why students were generally positive about their experiences with the CampusAware system. Analysis of the posted notes and survey results points to several possible answers. Use of CampusAware suggested that being in a particular environment reminds the user to contribute to the database based on this personal expertise. As one student commented, "If I saw something not on the program, I added it." Another participant posted a note that read, "Don't park on the road here. Tickets are $45.00." Seeing the location where the user received a parking ticket reminded him or her to post a note about the experience.

Authority or perceived expertise seemed to be the leading motivator for leaving notes. Over half of the participants answered that they had information that they did not find in the system or that they thought their views would be useful to future users. For example, users made comments like: "I thought I had some interesting points of views and additional information to contribute." Another user stated, "I felt it was important that others should be aware of certain things." Users seemed to desire to leave an opinion or share some knowledge.

This interpretation was indirectly corroborated when users left notes that related to buildings or spaces that they were unfamiliar with. Only about 9 percent of users posed questions of any kind. Part of the reason for this was inherent in the CampusAware design. Many who had questions didn't ask them because they wanted immediate feedback: "I can't get feedback quickly and effectively, and I like to ask questions on tours like this." This feedback issue points to an inherent disadvantage in a guided tour that is based on asynchronous communication. We are expanding our study to include perspective students in the future, with an eye toward investigating the role that familiarity plays as a mediating factor in usage.

MUSE: An Application

In looking at how portable electronic messaging devices are used in different contexts, we began to identify some common themes. Our latest efforts have been focused on developing a hand-held, contextually aware computer for a different context—museums. We began the design process by surveying our relevant social groups—in this case, museum administrators and curators, designers, and potential patrons. We used the cluster analysis technique that is described in chapter 2. Participants were asked to generate statements about usability, functionality, and any other information that they felt was important to the design. Differences appeared among the comments that were made by the three groups, but some overlap appeared in several areas. The top concerns for all three groups were artist information, functionality, and museum information. Thus our design has focused on these three issues.

MUSE is an interactive wireless network application that museum patrons can access through color personal digital assistants as they view various museum exhibits (figure 5.5). Works of art have infrared tags placed near them that broadcast a unique exhibit identification code that is read by the PDA and sent to a central server over the wireless network. The server responds with exhibit information that is presented as text, a rich mixture of audio, and images. In keeping with the notion that interaction and communication help create and define spaces, the MUSE application allows users to engage in discussions near various art pieces by writing and reading messages. Only a few users have tried the MUSE system as of this writing, but a full evaluation trial is planned in the near future.

Conclusion

The development of the MUSE interactive wireless network application was the culmination of four previous prototypes of context-aware applications for hand-held computing devices. Each prototype application was evaluated by users, whose comments helped us to better simulate and define relevant contextual features.

From this process, we derived a couple of design principles for context-aware computing. First, the device's context of use must be highly relevant to its users. Overly general contextual features can prevent users from understanding how the tool should function. The tool's purpose needs to be apparent and relevant before the user can benefit from its various contextual capabilities. This need for clarity was dramatically demonstrated when students appropriated the E-graffiti system as a chatting tool and ignored its location-specific communication features.

Second, users will readily contribute contextual information to a database when the context is highly relevant. As users of the campus-aware tour guide system contributed this information, contextual relevance and tool acceptance spiraled. In addition, the information that users contributed seems to be, in part, mediated by their level of familiarity with the context. Users of the CampusAware prototype posted few questions or

Figure 5.5
MUSE's interface

information-seeking notes, probably because they were already familiar with most of the locations and landmarks on campus. Our upcoming evaluations of CampusAware with prospective students and of MUSE with museum patrons will address this mediating influence of expertise more directly.

As the case studies presented in this chapter suggest, context seems to be indeed shaped by the activities that transpire in it, and those activities, in turn, shape the context of communication. Designs for context-aware tools, especially for mobile computing technologies, need to account for this fundamental, reciprocal relationship between context and activities. In the next chapter, we look at another important variable in designing for context-aware tools—the space that the context fills.

6

Configural Analysis of Spaces and Places

In earlier chapters in this book, we have discussed tool development, tool use (activity), and the context in which development and use occur. We have used case studies to illustrate our methodologies and findings and to show how those findings support different theoretical principles, particularly with respect to activity theory and its premises.

In this chapter, we discuss large datasets and position our case-study findings within a new theoretical framework. The large datasets that we examine represent different kinds of spaces and places, both virtual and real, large and small. Our aim is to begin thinking about and representing these spaces in ways that lead to seeing them as a collection of images in a ubiquitous computing family album.

The spaces that are represented in these datasets are varied: some are social networks, some are Web pages, and some are physical locations. Recent advances in visualization software packages allow us to "concretize" these otherwise ephemeral virtual spaces and thus treat them more as physical objects that we can look at, move, manipulate, and quantify. They have shape, size, attributes, and dimensions.

The challenge until recently has been to connect or link these different datasets conceptually and to begin thinking about ubiquitous computing as a whole rather than as compartmentalized behaviors and activities. A holistic approach would treat computing activities as integrated behaviors that contribute in varying degrees to the overall construct of ubiquitous computing. Although we have investigated how computing behaviors differ under various conditions, we also need to look at and understand similarities among different behaviors across a variety of computing environments.

This final chapter, then, focuses on ways to create structure within and across different spaces. Identifying patterns or regularities in and between these spaces is critical for building theories and designing spaces to support different computing activities. We have employed several techniques, some of which are explored in other chapters. Here we introduce a new lens with which to view various datasets. For this we borrow heavily from architecture theory, specifically configuration theory and the nondiscursive techniques that some in the field have applied to designing buildings, towns, and cities.

The natural overlap between physical and virtual spaces, the movement that takes place between these spaces, and the innate proclivity of humans to impose structure and meaning on these spaces seem too compelling to ignore. Analyzing these spaces by adopting architectural indices that are commonly used in planning and design might help us go beyond our current visualizations of data as representing "how things are" to how space "should be," which would optimize the intended use of the space.

Spaces as Physical Objects

We begin this chapter's study of space as the object of analysis—by looking simply at the layout or the grid itself and ignoring entirely the content of that space. Using various techniques, space as an object can be quantified in different ways to predict movement, flow, and interaction. In essence, these analytic techniques allow researchers to perform a pattern analysis that quantifies relationships among multiple spaces within a large space, such as the relationship among rooms within a floor plan. This kind of pattern analysis can lead to an understanding of the whole space. By identifying "nondiscursive regularities" (Hillier, 1996)—that is, spatial and formal patterns—we discover what is invariant in these patterns. The goal of configuration analysis is to extract these invariants to understand the whole from the relationships among its elemental units.

These regularities or patterns in spaces can reveal the social and cultural functioning in the space (Hillier, 1996). Because spatial layouts themselves convey certain information about function, there are "clear relationships between space patterns and how collections of people use them" (Hillier, 1996, p. 32).

We propose that investigation of computing behaviors in the various places and spaces in which they occur might benefit from a configurational analysis approach. If the form and configurational features of built environments convey information, present possibilities and limitations, and influence movement and behavior, then it seems likely that computing spaces, real or virtual, would impose similar influences and constraints. If we can represent these spaces in terms of their relational components, then we could borrow techniques from architecture that would allow us to quantify their configural properties and visually represent them accordingly. The ultimate goal is to amass enough data from different computing environments to begin to compare them and derive theoretical principles that may then be tested systematically.

Why Configuration Theory?

In thinking about things differently or in new ways, innovators often find it helpful, indeed necessary, to look for convergence or corroborating evidence that justifies breaking new ground. Configuration theory itself has been in the making for nearly twenty years, but its application in disciplines other than architecture has been a piecemeal practice at best.

Timing, necessity, and precedence have figured prominently in our decision to consider this new direction. The entire field of human-computer interaction has gone beyond the model of the sedentary user who creates a document in front of a stationary desktop computer. Users, uses, tools, and spaces are changing at a feverish pitch. In our own research, we have moved from evaluating a handful of people using a tool in a particular situation to collecting data on hundreds of people using myriad tools in dozens of locations and in countless different ways. We can no longer simply compare a few groups and look at performance differences between them. We need to look at very large datasets, which requires enormously powerful tools and complex ways of using those tools.

In recent years, techniques have been developed to graphically represent and visualize these large datasets that we find ourselves grappling with. Enormous strides have been made in the development of computer graphics, computer science, and software in general, which allow simple frequencies, means, and standard deviations to be pictorially represented

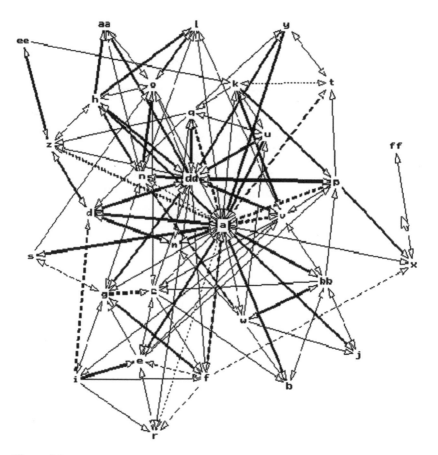

Figure 6.1
A social network analysis of e-mail traffic patterns

in meaningful ways. Now that we are able to better manage these large datasets, however, what can we really say about what we are now able to see? Take, for example, a social network analysis of e-mail correspondence among class members over a twenty-four-hour period (figure 6.1). This diagram shows that some e-mailers in this class are more central than others and that some are more peripheral. But in the absence of any other data that we might be able to correlate with e-mailers' network position, this visualization does not offer much explanatory or predictive power.

Representing data that have not been collected by controlling or manipulating some aspect in the setting is, at best, a snapshot aerial view of some larger landscape. Perhaps the data can be divided into some category (say, different groups of users), or perhaps the data were collected over time. Still, what can be said about any apparent differences—that group X's social network is different from group Y's or that social networks between time 1 and time 2 are different? Perhaps we simply haven't known what we want to be able to say. Staying with the example of the e-mailers, we envision being able to use configural analysis to suggest that social networks with configural attributes A, B, and C are predictive of outcomes or behaviors X, Y, and Z, but we need more than an aerial photograph to do this.

In addition to the analogy between built environments and computer spaces, another converging rationale supports this foray into the application of configuration theory in the analysis of computing spaces. As stated earlier, configuration theory is grounded on the premise that the relationships between elements within a space contribute to the overall functioning of that space more than any one element in isolation contributes. Cognitive and perceptual psychologists have long been concerned with how humans come to recognize objects, identify visual patterns, and construct cognitive maps of their external surroundings. From this diverse literature, we can find much in common with configuration theory. For example, from a Gibsonian perspective (see chapter 1), human perception is direct and immediate; all the information that humans need for perception is available in the spatial and surface layout of the immediate environment. We make sense of what we see not by interpreting some mediating cognitive process but by extracting invariant properties of objects and spaces from the multiple perspectives from which we view those objects and spaces. We deduce the structure, the capabilities, and the essence of a thing or space by identifying its recurrent, unchanging properties. The goal of configurational analysis is the detection of invariant patterns within and across spaces.

Relatedly, as Hillier (1996, p. 92) points out, the "human predilection for configuration" can also be noted in the structure of language. Like the behavioral outcomes that are generated by other abstract artifacts, "The words that make up speech and behaviors that seem social are all manifested in space-time sequences of dispositions of apparent elements whose interdependencies seem to be multiplex and irreducible to simple rules of combination." Paraphrasing from Chomsky, Hillier (1996, p. 91) continues, "Sentences . . . [are] a configurational proposition. Some degree of syncretic co-presence of many relations is involved whose nature cannot be reduced to an additive list of pairwise relations."

In addition to having a cognitive disposition for configuration and extraction, humans respond to the configural properties of a built environment, and those properties, in turn, affect how that built environment evolves as part of a more global complex. Hillier (1996, p. 153) suggests that responses to environment "seem to be governed by *pattern* laws of some kind" and that "there is a kind of natural geometry to what people do in spaces." Indeed, sociologists have spent years observing people in built environments and articulating hundreds of patterns for the design of healthy and vital environments (Alexander, 1977; Whyte, 1988). For example, in *City: Rediscovering the Center* (1988), William H. Whyte describes various patterns of human behavior that seem almost instinctual, unconscious, and archetypal. One of his examples—wall sitting—is a fascinating account of how people self-regulate the distribution of space for sitting along a ledge. As Whyte (1988, p. 127) comments, "It is as if people had some instinctive sense of what is right overall for a place and were cooperating to maintain it that way, obligingly leaving or sitting down, or not sitting, to keep the density within range."

Some have argued that the seeming lawfulness of these behaviors reflects some natural physical law or genetic predisposition. In fact, some architectural theories of building design and urban planning have exploited animal behavior patterns and animal biology. The underlying assumption of these approaches to design is that a built environment that reflects naturally occurring behavior patterns will result in greater harmony between form and function (Alberti, 1486/1988; Newman, 1971, 1972). Indeed, some support for this position has been found. Oscar Newman (1971, 1972) proposed that buildings and environments need to reflect humans' innate territoriality and instinct to defend individual space. He asserts that crime and other social ills can be accounted for, in part, by environmental design features that threaten the individual's ability to defend his or her territory. For example, increasing the height of a building (and thereby ignoring the need to keep density constant), can double the felony rate per 1,000 people in urban building projects.

Although much of the rationale for exploring configuration theory in the context of tool design is indirect, at the very least, configuration theory allows us to ask different design questions. Instead of studying the config-ural aspects of the space and asking, "What do people do in spaces?," we can ask, "Why do people do what they do in different spaces, and what configural patterns of the space foster those behaviors?"

Nondiscursive Techniques for Evaluating Space

In this section, we describe several techniques for evaluating the configural attributes of a space. Although an in-depth discussion of these techniques is beyond the scope of this chapter, we describe them here in general terms, apply them to general computer design issues, and use them to analyze a couple of large datasets.

In describing nondiscursive techniques for evaluating space, it seems useful to anchor them to the overarching goals for designing spaces and particularly for designing urban spaces. The first goal is *intelligibility*. Generally speaking, intelligent buildings and environments have been de-signed with the right spaces in the right relation to one another. *Right* in this context is discussed below. The second and necessarily related goal in designing spaces is good *local-to-global integration*—in other words, a strong relationship between the spaces' internal elements and the space as a whole. Both intelligibility and local-to-global integration figure promi-nently in the health or vitality of a space. Both also are useful as constructs in designing physical and virtual computing spaces.

Now the question becomes, "How are optimal levels of intelligibility and integration identified and achieved within a given space?" The funda-mental cornerstone in configural analysis is *depth* or the distance from one element in a space to all other elements in the space. Depth, as an in-dex, enables us to quantify the configural nature of a space.

Any space may be represented as a shape or a plan, which may then be visualized as a set of the shape's elements and the relationships of each ele-ment to each other element. A simple linear floor plan of, say, four rooms can be represented as four contiguous blocks (figure 6.2). The distance of each element to every other element can be calculated as shown in the figure. An integration value is derived from summing all the individual dis-tance values and is, in essence, a distance metric. Because this value repre-sents the sum of individual distances from one node or element to all

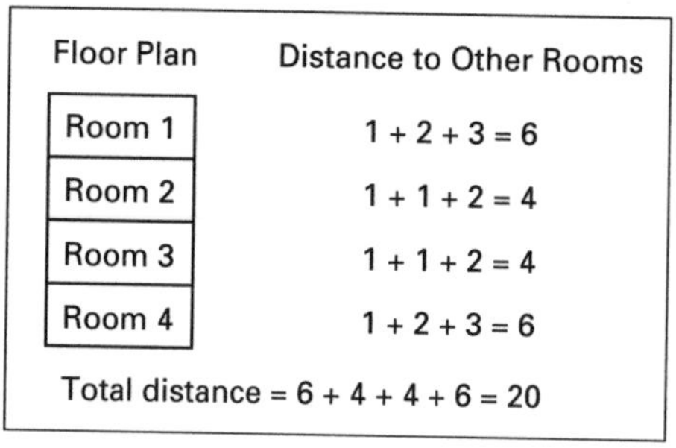

Floor Plan	Distance to Other Rooms
Room 1	1 + 2 + 3 = 6
Room 2	1 + 1 + 2 = 4
Room 3	1 + 1 + 2 = 4
Room 4	1 + 2 + 3 = 6
Total distance = 6 + 4 + 4 + 6 = 20	

Figure 6.2
A simple floor plan: individual distances and an integration value

others, Hillier (1996, p. 100) refers to it as a universal distance metric: the distribution of universal distances "represents the degree to which physical effort must be made to move from one part . . . to another."

Spaces can be analyzed from different perspectives—as arrangements of complex elements, such as hallways and rooms, or as overall shapes. Each analysis will yield different integration patterns and can be compared to reveal different aspects of functioning within the space. The resulting visual representations of the distribution of varying distances (or depths) can illustrate the space as gradations between well-integrated spaces and segregated spaces.

Well-integrated spaces are not necessarily intelligent spaces. Intelligibility is the relationship between what an individual can and cannot see from any given vantage point within the space. Connectivity is the amount of overlap that a space has with other spaces—specifically, the number of adjacent spaces that overlap and converge with a particular space. Integration—the total distance from a space to all other neighboring spaces—is, for the most part, not something that can be directly seen. Intelligent spaces allow us to make predictions about what we can't see based on what we do see locally. When integration values are plotted against connectivity, the data points for an intelligent space form a tight distribution around the regression line. This index of intelligibility is critical in designing urban spaces: because people cannot see all the adjoining spaces that make up the whole, some degree of prediction is extremely useful. Intelligibility is a useful index for software design as well as Web site design because it relates to the notion of navigation with the added benefit of being quantifiable.

Integration values can also be calculated to explore the relationship between local and global elements in the overall space, such as subareas of a city to its center. In urban design, local integration is related to small-scale movement (such as pedestrian traffic), whereas global integration relates to larger scale (such as vehicular movement). In essence, the two refer to different levels of movement—the former, internal movement, and the latter, movement in of and out of. To take advantage of these different levels of movements, cities create several interfaces between local levels of movement and large, global levels of movement.

The relationship between local and global elements underscores the importance of these two constructs of integration and intelligibility. It is what Hillier (1996, p. 142) refers to as the principle of natural movement—"the proportion of movement . . . that is determined by the structure of the urban grid itself, rather than by the presence of specific attractors or magnets." The structure of the space itself—the configural attributes that can be derived by these nondiscursive techniques—predicts movement patterns. When integration values are plotted against observed movement rates, the two are highly correlated. In other words, movement is the fundamental correlate of spatial configurations. This space-movement relationship is reciprocal, and more than any other feature within the space, it determines the effectiveness of urban spaces.

In a world of mobile ubiquitous computing, virtual information spaces, online communities, and simulations, these space and movement tools and theoretical premises might lend themselves to thinking about human computing behaviors. Spatial and building metaphors give us a vernacular for thinking about and designing spaces and also a way to represent them visually so that their underlying spatial patterns can be revealed. Movement happens in and between these virtual computing spaces, and movement patterns set the stage for the presence or absence of social interaction.

In our own research, we are both challenged and intrigued by configuration theory and these techniques. Some of our existing datasets fold or map easily onto these techniques. For example, as part of a larger mobile computing project (the CampusAware system, which is described in chapter 4), we tracked users' locations across the Cornell campus as they used

Figure 6.3
Campus map showing wireless network traffic patterns

the wireless network. Figure 6.3 shows a map of the Cornell campus that is overlaid with users' wireless network access points (the lines between buildings indicate transitions from one location to another). These data can then be represented as a map or grid and analyzed for integration and connectivity. One question that we have is whether the spatial layout of the wireless network predicts mobile computing patterns. We also might ask how the space-movement relationship in the wireless networking environment overlaps with general space-movement patterns across the campus. Similarly, using the social network analysis of e-mail traffic patterns that are mentioned earlier in this chapter, we can represent strong and weak ties as axial maps, obtain integration values for the distances between lines, and look at the resulting patterns of local-to-global integration to see whether they predict certain other outcomes, such as technology or tool adoption.

Finally, we intend to explore how these techniques might be applied to our eye-tracking research. Web pages and their corresponding look zones or areas of interest can be represented spatially (figure 6.4). At the top of figure 6.4 is a Web page layout with the path taken by a user's eye across

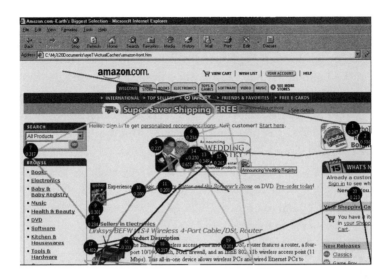

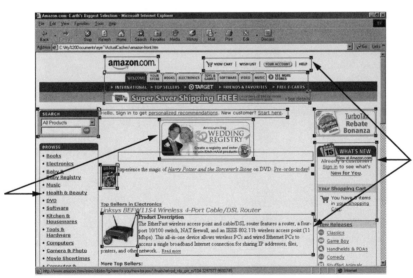

Figure 6.4
Scan paths and look zones for an Amazon front page

the page. Below this, look zones are designated for different areas of interest. Hypothetically, at least, this space could be analyzed much like the complex elements within a house floor plan, with look zones as rooms within the building and spaces between them representing hallways and corridors. Again, integration values for different zones within and across pages could be obtained, and eye movements and scan paths could be correlated with them. The space-movement relationship in this area might then be correlated with navigation.

Looking for similar movement patterns among and even between these different spaces, real and virtual, large and small, is our ultimate goal at this time. The potential of these techniques in their application to investigations in human-computer interaction however, is bounded only by the spaces that we decide to explore.

References

Abowd, G., & Mynatt, E. (2000, March). Charting past, present, and future research in ubiquitous computing. *ACM Transactions on Computer-Human Interaction, 7*(1), 29–58.

Abowd, G., Pimentel, M., Kerimbaev, B., Ishiguro, Y., & Guzdial, M. (1999). Anchoring discussions in lecture: An approach to collaboratively extending classroom digital media. *Proceedings of the Computer Support for Collaborative Learning (CSCL) 1999 Conference* (pp. 11–19). Palo Alto: Stanford University Press.

Alberti, L. B. (1988). *On the art of building in ten books* (J. Rykwert, N. Leach, & R. Tavernor, Trans.). Cambridge, MA: MIT Press. (Original work published 1486)

Alexander, C. (1977). *A pattern language.* New York: Oxford University Press.

Baker, M., Hansen, T., Joiner, R., & Traum, D. (1999). The role of grounding in collaborative learning tasks. In P. Dillenbourg (Ed.), *Collaborative learning: Cognitive and computational approaches* (pp. 31–63). Amsterdam: Pergamon.

Bannon, L. (1989). Issues in computer-supported collaborative learning. In C. O'Malley (Ed.), *Computer supported collaborative learning* (pp. 267–282). Berlin: Springer-Verlag.

Bell, G. (1999). The museum as cultural ecology: A study. CIMI whitepapers. Retrieved February 20, 2003, from <http://www.cimi.org/publications.html>.

Bijker, W., & Law, J. (Eds.). (1992). *Shaping technology/building society: Studies in sociotechnical change.* Cambridge, MA: MIT Press.

Black, S. D., Levin, J. A., Mehan, H., & Quinn, C. N. (1983). Real and non-real time interaction: Unraveling multiple threads of discourse. *Discourse Processes, 6,* 59–75.

Blacker, F., Crump, N., & McDonald, S. (1999). Managing experts and competing through innovation. *Organization, 6*(1), 5–31.

Blacker, F., Crump, N., & McDonald, S. (2000). Organizing processes in complex activity networks. *Organization, 7*(2), 277–300.

Bødker, S. (1997). Computers in mediated human activity. *Mind, Culture, and Activity, 4*(3), 149–158.

Bødker, S., & Petersen, M. G. (2000). Design for learning in use. *Scandinavian Journal of Information Systems, 12,* 61–80.

Boer, N., Van Baalen, P., & Kumar, K. (2002). An activity theory approach for studying the dynamics of knowledge sharing. *Proceedings of the Thirty-fifth Annual Hawaii International Conference on System Sciences (HICSS 35)* (pp. 90–93). Los Alamitos, CA: IEEE Computer Society Press.

Bronfenbrenner, U. (1979). *The ecology of human development.* Cambridge, MA: Harvard University Press.

Bronfenbrenner, U. (1989). Ecological systems theory. *Annals of Child Development, 6,* 187–249.

Burrell, J., & Gay, G. (2001). Collectively defining context in a mobile, networked computing environment. In *Extended Abstracts of Computer-Human Interaction (CHI) 2001* (pp. 231–232). New York: ACM Press.

Burrell, J., Treadwell, P., & Gay, G. (2000). Designing for context: Usability in a ubiquitous environment. *Conference on Universal Usability: 2000 Proceedings* (pp. 80–84). New York: ACM Press.

Butler, K. (1996). Usability engineering turns ten. *IEEE Interactions, 3*(1), 59–75.

Carr, D. (1999, March–April). The need for the museum. *Museum News, 78*(2), 31–35.

Cho, H., Stefanone, M., & Gay, G. (2002). Social information sharing in a CSCL community. *Proceedings of the Computer Support for Collaborative Learning (CSCL) 2002 Conference.* Palo Alto: Stanford University Press.

Clark, H. H. (1996). *Using language.* Cambridge: Cambridge University Press.

Clark, H. H., & Brennan, S. E. (1991). Grounding in communication. In L. B. Resnick, J. Levine, & S. D. Teasley (Eds.), *Perspectives on socially shared cognition* (pp. 127–149). Washington, DC: American Psychological Association.

Crook, C. (1989). Educational practice within two local computer networks. In C. O'Malley (Ed.), *Computer-supported collaborative learning* (pp. 165–182). Berlin: Springer-Verlag.

Crook, C. (1994). *Computers and the Collaborative experience of learning.* London: Routledge.

Dennis, A. R., George, J. F., Jessup, L. M., Nunamaker, J. F., & Vogel, D. R. (1988). Information technology to support electronic meetings. *MIS Quarterly, 12,* 591–624.

Dey, A. K., Abowd, G. D., & Salber, D. (2001). A conceptual framework and toolkit for supporting the rapid prototyping of context-aware applications. *Journal of Human-Computer Interaction, Special Issue, 16*(2), 97–166.

Dieberger, A. (1999). Social navigation in populated information spaces: Social connotations of space. In A. Munro, K. Höök, & D. Benyon (Eds.), *Social navigation of information space* (pp. 35–54). London: Springer.

Dillenbourg, P. (Ed.). (1999). *Collaborative learning: Cognitive and computational approaches*. Amsterdam: Pergamon.

Douglas, S. (1987). *Inventing American broadcasting, 1899–1922.* Baltimore: Johns Hopkins University Press.

Dufresne-Tassé, C. (1995). Andragogy (adult education) in the museum: A critical analysis and new formulation. In E. Hooper-Greenhill (Ed.), *Museum, media, message* (pp. 245–259). New York: Routledge.

Edwards, P. (1995). Computers in society and culture. In S. Jasanoff (Ed.), *Handbook of science and technology studies* (pp. 212–263). Thousand Oaks, CA: Sage.

Ehn, P. (1988). *Work-oriented design of computer artifacts.* Hillsdale, NJ: Erlbaum.

Engeström, Y. (1999a). Activity theory and individual and social transformation. In Y. Engeström, R. Miettinen, & R. Punamäki (Eds.), *Perspectives on activity theory* (pp. 19–38). Cambridge: Cambridge University Press.

Engeström, Y. (1999b). Innovative learning in work teams: Analyzing cycles of knowledge creation in practice. In Y. Engeström, R. Miettinen, & R. Punamäki (Eds.), *Perspectives on activity theory* (pp. 377–404). Cambridge: Cambridge University Press.

Engeström, Y. (1999c). *Learning by expanding: An activity theoretical approach to developmental research.* Helsinki: Orenta-Konsultit.

Engeström, Y., Miettinen, R., & Punamäki, R. (Eds.). (1999). *Perspectives on activity theory.* Cambridge: Cambridge University Press.

Erickson, T., Halverson, C., Kellogg, W., Laff, M., & Wolf, T. (2002, April). Social translucence: Designing social infrastructures that make collective activity visible. *Communications of the ACM, 45*(4), 43–56.

Evans, G. (1995). Learning and the physical environment. In J. H. Falk & L. Dierking (Eds.), *Public institutions for personal learning: Establishing a research agenda* (pp. 119–126). Washington, DC: American Association of Museums.

Finlay, I. (1977). *Priceless heritage: The future of museums.* London: Faber and Faber.

Fulk, J. (1993). Social construction of communication technology. *Academy of Management Journal, 36*(5), 921–950.

Garfinkel, H. (1967). *Studies in ethnomethodology.* New York: Prentice-Hall.

Garfinkel, H., & Sacks, H. (1970). The formal practices of practical actions. In J. C. McKinney & E. A. Tiryakian (Eds.), *Theoretical sociology* (pp. 338–366). New York: Appleton-Century-Crofts.

Gay, G., & Bennington, T. (1999). *Information technologies in evaluation: Social, moral, epistemological, and practical implications.* San Francisco: Jossey-Bass.

Gay, G., & Bennington, T. (2003). *Blurring boundaries: A study of ubiquitous computing.* Paper presented at the Fifty-third Annual Conference of the International Communication Association, San Diego, May 23–27.

Gay, G., Boehner, K., & Panella, T. (1997). ArtView: Transforming image databases into collaborative learning spaces. *Educational Computing Research, 16*(4), 317–332.

Gay, G., & Hembrooke, H. (2002). Browsing behaviors in wireless learning networks. In *Proceedings of the Thirty-fifth Annual Hawaii International Conference on System Sciences* (pp. 33–35). Los Alamitos, CA: IEEE Computer Society Press.

Gay, G., & Lentini, M. (1995). Use of communication resources in a networked collaborative design environment. *Journal of Computer-Mediated Communication, 1*(1). Retrieved February 23, 2003, from <http://cwis.usc.edu/dept/annenberg .vol1/issue1/contents.html>.

Gay, G., Reiger, R., & Bennington, T. (2002). Using mobile computing to enhance field study. In N. Miyake, R. Hall, & T. Koschmann (Eds.), *Carrying the conversation forward* (pp. 414–528). Mahwah, NJ: Erlbaum.

Gay, G., & Stefanone, M. (2002). Handheld access to the digital landscape. Retrieved January 12, 2003, from <http://www.cimi.org/public_docs/ps1_write_up4 .html>.

Gay, G., Stefanone, M., Grace-Martin, M., & Hembrooke, H. (2002). The effects of wireless computing in collaborative learning environments. *International Journal of Human-Computer Interaction, 3,* 35–42.

Gay, G., Sturgill, A., Martin, W., & Huttenlocher, D. (1999). Document-centered peer collaborations: An exploration of the educational uses of networked communication technologies. *Journal of Computer-Mediated Communication 4*(3). Retrieved February 23, 2003, from <http://www.ascusc.org/jcmc/vol4/issue3/>.

Gibson, J. J. (1977). The theory of affordances. In R. Shaw & J. Bransford (Eds.), *Perceiving, acting, and knowing* (pp. 171–198). Hillsdale, NJ: Erlbaum.

Gibson, J. J. (1979). *The ecological approach to visual perception.* Boston: Houghton Mifflin.

Gifford, B. R., & Enyedy, N. D. (1999). Activity-centered design: Towards a theoretical framework for CSCL. In *Proceedings of the Computer Support for Collaborative Learning (CSCL) 1999 Conference* (pp. 189–196). Palo Alto: Stanford University Press.

Goffman, E. (1959). *The presentation of self in everyday life.* New York: Doubleday Anchor.

Goffman, E. (1974). Frame analysis: An essay on the organization of experience. New York: Harper and Row.

Goodwin, C., & Heritage, J. (1986). Conversation analysis. *Annual Review of Anthropology, 19,* 283–307.

Grace-Martin, M., & Gay, G. (2001). Web browsing, mobile computing and academic performance. *IEEE and International Forum of Educational Technology & Society, 4,* 143–164.

Greenberg, S. (2001). Context as a dynamic construct. *Journal of Human-Computer Interaction, Special Issue, 16*(2), 257–268.

Grudin, J. (1988). Why CSCW applications fail: Problems in the design and evaluation of organizational interfaces. *Proceedings of the 1988 ACM Conference on Computer-Supported Cooperative Work (CSCW)* (pp. 85–93). Retrieved March 14, 2002, from <http://portal.acm.org>.

Hancock, J. T., & Dunham, P. J. (2001). Language use in computer-mediated communication: The role of coordination devices. *Discourse Processes, 31,* 91–110.

Hasan, H., Gould, E., & Hyland, P. (Eds.). (1998). *Information systems and activity theory: Tools in context.* Wollongong: University of Wollongong Press.

Heidegger, M. (1962). *Being and time.* San Francisco: Harper.

Hein, H. S. (2000). *The museum in transition: A philosophical perspective.* Washington, DC: Smithsonian Press.

Herring, S. C. (1996). Two variants of an electronic message schema. In S. C. Herring (Ed.), *Computer-mediated communication: Linguistic, social, and cross-cultural perspectives* (pp. 81–108). Philadelphia: Benjamins.

Herring, S. C. (1999). Interactional coherence in CMC. *Journal of Computer-Mediated Communication, 4*(4). Retrieved February 23, 2003, from <http://www.ascusc.org/jcmc/vol4/issue4/herring.html>.

Hillier, B. (1996). *Space is the machine.* Cambridge: Cambridge University Press.

Hoadley, C. M., & Enyedy, N. (1999). Between information and communication: Middle spaces in computer media for learning. *Proceedings of the Computer Support for Collaborative Learning (CSCI) 1999 Conference* (pp. 242–251). Palo Alto: Stanford University Press.

Hooper-Greenhill, E. (2000). *Museums and the interpretation of visual culture.* New York: Routledge.

Ihde, D. (1991). *Instrumental realism: The interface between philosophy of science and philosophy of technology.* Bloomington: Indiana University Press.

Kaptelinin, V. (1996). Activity theory: Implications for human-computer interaction. In B. A. Nardi (Ed.), *Context and consciousness: Activity theory and human-computer interaction* (pp. 103–117). Cambridge, MA: MIT Press.

Kaptelinin, V., Nardi, B., & Macaulav, C. (1999, July–August). The activity checklist: A tool for representing the "space" of context. *Interactions,* 29–36.

Keene, S. (1998). *Digital collections: Museums and the information age.* Oxford: Butterworth-Heinemann.

Kilker, J., & Gay, G. (1998, June). The social construction of a digital library: A case study examining implications for evaluation. *Information Technology and Libraries,* 60–70.

Koschmann, T. (Ed.). (1996). *CSCL: Theory and practice of an emerging paradigm.* Mahwah, NJ: Erlbaum.

Kotler, N., & Kotler, P. (1998). *Museum strategy and marketing.* San Francisco: Jossey-Bass.

Kuutti, K. (1996). Activity theory as a potential framework for human-computer interaction research. In B. A. Nardi (Ed.), *Context and consciousness: Activity theory and human-computer interaction* (pp. 17–45). Cambridge, MA: MIT Press.

Latour, B. (1987). *Science in action.* Cambridge, MA: Harvard University Press.

Lave, J., & Wenger, E. (1991). Legitimate peripheral participation in communities of practice. In *Situated learning: Legitimate peripheral participation.* Cambridge: Cambridge University Press.

Leont'ev, A. N. (1978). *Activity, consciousness, and personality.* Englewood Cliffs, NJ: Prentice-Hall.

Leont'ev, A. N. (1981). *Problems of the development of mind.* Moscow: Progress.

Levy, D., & Marshall, C. (1995). Going digital: A look at assumptions underlying digital libraries. *Communications of the ACM, 38*(4), 77–84.

Light, P., & Light, V. (1999). Analysing asynchronous interaction: Computer mediated communication in a conventional undergraduate setting. In K. Littleton & P. Light (Eds.), *Learning with computers: Analysing productive interaction.* London: Routledge.

Mark, W. (1999). Turning pervasive computing into mediated spaces. *IBM Systems Journal, 38*(4), 677–692.

Mead, J., & Gay, G. (1995) Concept mapping: An Innovative approach to digital library design and evaluation. Retrieved March 3, 2002, from <http://edfu.lis.uicu.edu/allerton/95/s2/mead/mead.html>.

Mehan, H., & Wood, H. (1975). *The reality of ethnomethodology.* New York: Wiley.

Mintz, A. (1998). Media and museums: A museum perspective. In S. Thomas & A. Mintz (Eds.), *The virtual and the real: Media in the museum* (pp. 19–34). Washington, DC: American Association of Museums.

Morrissey, K., & Worts, D. (1998). A place for the muses? Negotiating the role of technology in museums. In S. Thomas & A. Mintz (Eds.), *The virtual and the real:*

Media in the museum (pp. 147–171). Washington, DC: American Association of Museums.

Munro, A. J., Hook, K., & Benyon, D. (Eds.). (1999). *Social navigation of information space.* New York: Springer Verlag.

Nardi, B. A. (1996a). Activity theory and human-computer interaction. In B. A. Nardi (Ed.), *Context and consciousness: Activity theory and human-computer interaction* (pp. 7–16). Cambridge, MA: MIT Press.

Nardi, B. A. (1996b). *Context and consciousness: Activity theory and human-computer interaction.* Cambridge, MA: MIT Press.

Nardi, B., & O'Day, V. (1999). *Information ecologies: Using technologies with heart.* Cambridge, MA: MIT Press.

Nardi, B. A., Schwartz, H., Kuchinsky, A., Leichner, R., Whittaker, S., & Sclabassi, R. (1993). Turning away from talking heads: The use of video-as-data in neurosurgery. *InterCHI 93 Conference Proceedings Conference on Human Factors in Computing Systems* (pp. 327–335). Reading, MA: Addison Wesley.

Newman, O. (1971). *Architectural design for crime prevention.* Washington, DC: U.S. Department of Justice, National Institute of Law Enforcement and Criminal Justice.

Newman, O. (1972). *Defensible space.* New York: Macmillan.

Norman, D. A. (1983). Some observations on mental models. In D. Genter & A. L. Stevens (Eds.), *Mental models* (pp. 7–14). Hillsdale, NJ: Erlbaum.

Norman, D. A. (1988). *The design of everyday things.* New York: Doubleday.

Norman, D. A. (1998). *The invisible computer: Why good products can fail, the personal computer is so complex, and information appliances are the solution.* Cambridge, MA: MIT Press.

Pascoe, J. (1997). The stick-e note architecture: Extending the interface beyond the user. *Proceedings of the 1997 International Conference on Intelligent User Interfaces* (pp. 261–264). New York: ACM Press.

Pettigrew, A. (1990). Longitudinal field research on change theory and practice. *Organization Science, 1,* 267–292.

Pinch, T., & Bijker, W. (1987). The social construction of facts and artifacts: Or how the sociology of science and the sociology of technology might benefit each other. In W. Bijker, T. Hughes, & T. Pinch (Eds.), *The social construction of technological systems: New directions in the sociology and history of technology* (pp. 17–50). Cambridge, MA: MIT Press.

Schegloff, E. A. (1991). Conversation analysis and socially shared cognition. In L. Resnick, J. Levine, & S. D. Bernard (Eds.), *Socially shared cognition* (pp. 150–172). Washington, DC: American Psychological Association.

Schegloff, E. A., & Sacks, H. (1973). Opening up closings. *Semiotica, 7,* 289–327.

Schorr, A. (1995). The quick response center: An interactive business learning environment. *Interpersonal Computing and Technology, 3*(4), 57–65.

Suchman, L. (1987). *Plans and situated actions: The problem of human-machine communication.* Cambridge, MA: Harvard University Press.

Sugita, S., Hong, J.-K., Reeve, J., & Gay, G. (Eds.). (2002). *Global digital museum (GDM) for museum education on the Internet.* Osaka, Japan: National Museum of Ethnology.

Thomas, S. (1998). Introduction. In S. Thomas & A. Mintz (Eds.), *The virtual and the real: Media in the museum* (pp. viii–xi). Washington, DC: American Association of Museums.

Tolmie, A., & Boyle, J. (2000). Factors influencing the success of computer-mediated communication (CMC) environments in university teaching: A review and case study. *Computers & Education, 34,* 119–140.

Trochim, W. (1985). Pattern matching, validity, and conceptualization. *Evaluation Review, 9,* 575–604.

Trochim, W., & Linton, R. (1986). Conceptualization for evaluation and planning. *Evaluation and Program Planning, 9,* 289–308.

Vygotsky, L. (1962). *Thought and language.* Cambridge, MA: MIT Press.

Webb, N. M. (1989). Peer interaction and learning in small groups. *International Journal of Educational Research, 13,* 21–39.

Well, S. E. (1990). *Rethinking the museum, and other meditations.* London: Smithsonian Institution Press.

Wenger, E. (1998). *Communities of practice: Learning, meaning, and identity.* Cambridge: Cambridge University Press.

Wertsch, J. W. (Ed.). (1991). *Voice of the mind: A sociocultural approach to mediated activity.* Cambridge, MA: Harvard University Press.

Whyte, W. H. (1988). *City: Rediscovering the center.* New York: Doubleday.

Winograd, T. (2001). Architectures for context. *Journal of Human-Computer Interaction* (special issue), *16(2),* 401–419.

Index